2nd INTERNATIONAL CONFERENCE 2024
on
NEW TRENDS & MODERN APPROCHES IN EDUCATION

CONFERENCE SOUVENIR

Editor -In-Chief

Dr. Shivakumar G S., Principal

Editors

Dr. Devaraja Y., Assistant Professor
Dr. Kiran Kumar K S., Assistant Professor
Dr. Vani Nayaki D C., Assistant Professor
Sri. Vishwanatha G., Librarian

Co-Editors

Dr. Veerendrakumar Wali S., Assistant Professor
Dr. Ravi H., Assistant Professor
Dr. Yadukumar M., Assistant Professor
Sri. Nagendrappa S., Assistant Professor
Sri. Ravi Kumar N G., Physical Education Director

A Compilation of paper abstracts presented in Two days International National Conference:

NEW TRENDS & MODERN APPROCHES IN EDUCATION

Edited by: Dr. Shivakumar G. S., Dr. Devaraja Y., Dr. Kiran Kumar K S. Dr. Vani Nayaki D C. & Sri. Vishwanatha G.

Published by : Notion Press Publication No.8, 3rd Cross St, CIT Colony Mylapore, Chennai, Tamil Nadu 600004
Email ID: publish@notionpress.com
Phone : 044 4631 5631

Pages : 19+104 = 123

Price : 285=00 /-

First published : October 18th &19th, 2024

ISBN : 979-889588149-1

Rights and Permission : ©2024 Kumadvathi College of Education, Shikaripura

Disclaimer: "The views expressed in the articles/research papers are of the respective authors /researchers".

ORGANISING COMMITTEE

CHIEF PATRON

Sri. B.S. YEDDIYURAPPA
Founder Chairman
Swamy Vivekananda Vidya Samsthe (R),
Shikaripura &

PATRON

Sri. B.Y. RAGHAVENDRA
Secretary
Swamy Vivekananda Vidya Samsthe (R),
Shikaripura &
Member of Parliament, Shivamogga Constituency

Sri. B.Y. VIJAYENDRA
Treasurer
Swamy Vivekananda Vidya Samsthe (R), Shikaripura &
Member of Legislative Assembly, Shikaripura
Constituency

ADVISORY COMMITTEE

Sri. SHIVAKUMAR M B
President
Swamy Vivekananda Vidya Samsthe (R)
Shikaripura

Smt. TEJASWINI RAGHAVENDRA
Director
Swamy Vivekananda Vidya Samsthe (R)
Shikaripura

Smt. PREMA VIJAYENDRA
Director
Swamy Vivekananda Vidya Samsthe (R)
Shikaripura

Smt. S.Y UMADEVI
Governing Council Member
PESITM, Shivamogga

Sri. SUBHASH B R
Governing Council Member
Swamy Vivekananda Vidya Samsthe
Shikaripura

CONFERENCE DIRECTOR

Dr. SHIVAKUMAR G S
Principal, Kumadvathi College of Education &
Management Representative of SVVS

ORGANISING SECRETARIES

Dr. DEVARAJA Y
Assistant Professor
Kumadvathi College of Education

Dr. KIRAN KUMAR K S
Assistant Professor
Kumadvathi College of Education

CONVENORS

Dr. VANINAYAKI D.C
Assistant Professor

MR. VISHWANATH G
Librarian

ORGANISING MEMBERS

Dr. VEERENDRAKUMAR WALI S
Assistant Professor

Dr. YADUKUMAR M
Assistant Professor

Dr. RAVI H
Assistant Professor

Mr. NAGENDRAPPA S
Assistant Professor

Mr. RAVIKUMARA N G
Physical Education Director

INDEX

Sl No	Name of the Contributors	Title of the Paper	Page No
1	Dr. Sheikh Tahmina Awal & Dr. S M Hafizur Rahman	Exploring the emphasis of employability skills and values development in Botany curriculums across public universities in Bangladesh	2
2	Dr. Rezina Ahmed & Dr. S M Hafizur Rahman	Teachers' understanding on science process skills of primary science teaching practice in Bangladesh: rural and urban perspectives	3
3	Owuor Paul Felix, Dr Aden Ali Abdi & Dr Robert Machyo	Educational Paradigm Shift: Linking School Conditions to Student Transition in Garissa Township Sub-County, Kenya.	4
4	Dr. Shivakumar G S	Empowering Education Through Innovation	5
5	Dr. Shivakumar G S	Education in 2050: A Vision for the Future	5-6
6	Dr.Devaraja Y	Study of Values of Secondary School Students in Relation to Modernization	6
7	Dr.Devaraja Y	Education, Technology and Peace – Promoting World Peace	7
8	Dr. Veerendra Kumar Wali S.	A Comparative Study on Reading Habits of Underachievers in Academic Achievement of Secondary School Students	7-8
9	Dr. Yadukumar M	Leadership Behaviour among Student Teachers (B.Ed. Trainees)	8-9
10	Dr. Yadukumar M	The Influence of Lifestyle on Academic Performance among Student Teachers	9-10

Principal's Message

It is with great pride and enthusiasm that I welcome all distinguished guests, researchers, educators, and participants to the 2nd International Conference on "New Trends & Modern Approaches in Education." This conference, centered around innovative practices in education, is a testament to the evolving nature of teaching and learning in the 21st century.

The compilation of abstracts that has been prepared for this conference represents the cutting edge of thought in the educational arena. These abstracts serve as a window into the pioneering work of scholars and practitioners from around the world. Each one reflects not only the dedication and expertise of the authors but also the diverse approaches being explored to enhance educational outcomes.

From integrating technology and modern pedagogical methods to addressing equity, inclusion, and lifelong learning, the abstracts highlight critical discussions that promise to shape the future of education. These brief but insightful summaries encapsulate the research that will drive our conversations forward, fostering an exchange of ideas that is essential for progress.

I encourage all attendees to engage deeply with the presentations and discussions that will emerge from these abstracts. It is through these scholarly contributions that we can collectively explore and identify new pathways for innovation and improvement in education.

I wish all contributors and participants the very best as we embark on this exciting intellectual journey. May this conference inspire fruitful dialogues and open up new avenues for collaboration in the global educational community.

Best regards,

Dr. Shivakumar G S

Principal, Kumadvathi College of Education,
Shikaripura, & Management Represetative, SVVS,
& Conference Director.

Message from Editorial Board

We welcome you to the 2nd International Conference on New Trends and Modern Approaches in Education with great enthusiasm. This prestigious event provides a vital platform for researchers, educators, and practitioners from across the globe to come together, share insights, and explore the evolving landscape of education.

In today's rapidly changing world, education plays a pivotal role in shaping the future. The conference theme underscores the importance of embracing innovative trends and adopting modern methodologies to meet the demands of 21st-century learners. As we navigate challenges like technological advancement, diverse learning needs, and global interconnectedness, we must reimagine how we teach, learn, and engage.

This year's conference offers a wide array of presentations and discussions on topics ranging from digital learning platforms and personalized education to sustainable teaching practices and equity in education. The diversity of perspectives and experiences represented by our esteemed speakers and attendees enriches our collective understanding and drives meaningful change in the field.

We believe that the ideas exchanged during this conference will inspire new strategies, foster collaboration, and ultimately lead to more impactful and inclusive educational practices worldwide. We look forward to the insightful discussions, networking opportunities, and innovative solutions that will emerge from this gathering.

Thank you for joining us in this journey toward a more dynamic and forward-thinking approach to education. Together, we can pave the way for a brighter, more equitable future for learners everywhere.

Sincerely,

Dr. Devaraja Y
Assistant Professor, & Organising Secretary
Kumadvathi College of Education,
Shikaripura

Dr. Kiran Kumar K S
Assistant Professor, & Organising Secretary
Kumadvathi College of Education,
Shikaripura

Message from IQAC

Kumadvathi College of Education, Shikaripura. The IQAC being an integral part of the college works towards realizing the goals of quality enhancement by developing a system for conscious, consistent and catalytic improvement in different aspects of functioning of the college.

The IQAC assures the stakeholders i.e., researchers, students, parents, teachers, staff, management, funding agencies, Alumni's and society in general – of the accountability and transparency in the quality management system of the institution and its concern for ensuring quality of education being imparted.

The IQAC of KCE, organises various programmes for faculty, administrative staff and quality circle members. It conducts open forum to provide interface between students and staff. It conducts staff assessment to provide valuable feedback for quality sustenance and improvement in teaching, learning and research experiences in the college. It documents and reports various activities of the college for various higher education requirements. A continuous follow up has been made on infrastructural resources of the college to assure adequate, appropriate and better facilities to assure conducive and enabling environment for teaching, learning and research. Through all these measures IQAC happens to be one of the important components of the college which ensures quality and continuous improvement in all the aspects of the college.

The conference on **"New Trends & Modern Approaches in Education"** serves as a pivotal gathering for educators, researchers, policymakers, and industry experts who are passionate about shaping the future of education. This conference provides a platform to explore and discuss the latest developments and innovative practices in the field.

I wish all deligates, researchers, Students and participants the very best as we get on this exciting intellectual journey. May this International conference inspire fruitful discussions and open up new avenues for collaboration in the worldwide educational community.

With Best Wishes.

Dr. Ravi H.,
Assistant Professor and IQAC Co-ordinator
Kumadvathi College of Education, Shikaripura

About the Conference

The conference on "New Trends & Modern Approaches in Education" serves as a pivotal gathering for educators, researchers, policymakers, and industry experts who are passionate about shaping the future of education. This conference provides a platform to explore and discuss the latest developments and innovative practices in the field.

A new trend within an educational system can be seen as a shift that may potentially influence how the system functions. These shifts could include new teaching methods, changes in research and curriculum development, as well as evolving attitudes and behaviours among staff and students. Educational trends might present themselves as threats, challenges, opportunities, innovations, or initiatives that contribute to the social, economic, political, and cultural development of society.

Modern trends in educational development drive changes and create conditions necessary for innovations in teaching, learning, administration, research, and community services on a global scale. Examples of these trends include social learning, learning design informed by analytics, flipped classrooms, dynamic assessment, and event-based learning. The evolving global economy and advancements in modern technologies have ushered in new trends aimed at enhancing global competitiveness in education. These modern trends emphasize innovation, accessibility, and adaptability, promoting positive global change. As a result, students are encouraged to learn through interactive and practical tools that foster knowledge-building and productivity, helping them compete globally with practical knowledge that supports their personal and professional growth.

OBJECTIVES OF THE CONFERENCE

- Provide a platform for researchers, educators, and practitioners to share the latest research findings, innovative teaching methods, and successful case studies.

- Showcase the latest educational technologies and their applications in enhancing teaching and learning processes.

- Identify and discuss emerging trends in education that could shape the future of teaching and learning.

- Promote inclusivity and diversity in education by discussing strategies to create equitable learning environments for all students.

THEMES & SUB-THEMES OF THE CONFERENCE

1. **Emerging Educational Technologies**
- Integration of AI and Machine Learning in Education
- Virtual Reality (VR) and Augmented Reality (AR) in the classroom
- Blockchain in Educational Credentialing
- Internet of Things (IoT) for Smart Learning Environments
- Educational Apps and Mobile Learning
- Educational Robotics and Coding

2. **Innovative Pedagogical Strategies & Digital Transformation in Education**
- Flipped Classroom Models
- Gamification in Education
- Inquiry-Based Learning Approaches
- Project-Based Learning (PBL)
- Personalized and Adaptive Learning Systems
- E-Learning Platforms and Online Course Development
- Digital Assessment Tools and Techniques
- Technology-Enhanced Assessment
- Implementing Blended Learning
- Challenges and Opportunities in Digital Education
- Ensuring Quality in Online Learning

3. **Social and Emotional Learning (SEL)**
- Integrating SEL into the Curriculum
- Mindfulness and Well-Being in Education
- Developing Emotional Intelligence
- SEL Programs and Their Impact
- Role of SEL in Student Success

4. **Future Trends in Education & Teachers' Professional Development**
- Predicting the Future of Education
- Globalization and Education
- Preparing Students for the Future Workforce
- Continuous Professional Learning and Development
- Digital Literacy for Educators
- Innovative Teaching Practices and Methodologies
- Teacher Leadership and Mentorship
- Reflective Practice in Teaching

5) **Curriculum Innovation and Design**
- STEAM Education
- Interdisciplinary and Transdisciplinary Curriculum Approaches
- Culturally Responsive Teaching Practices
- Competency-Based Education Models
- Curriculum Mapping and Alignment

6. **Future of Education**
- NEP-2020: Challenges & Opportunities
- Trends Shaping the Future of Education
- Preparing Students for Future Careers
- Lifelong Learning and Adult Education
- Future Skills and Competencies
- Recent trends and concepts in Sports, Physical & Health Education
- Yoga in Education
- Digital Libraries & Repositories
- Moocs & OERs
- Business Industry and Economics of Education
- Language Education and Literacy
- Inclusive Learning & Special Education

Exploring the emphasis of employability skills and values development in Botany curriculums across public universities in Bangladesh

Dr. Sheikh Tahmina Awal

Associate Professor, Institute of Education and Research, University of Dhaka, Bangladesh, Email: stawal@du.ac.bd

Dr. S M Hafizur Rahman

Professor, Institute of Education and Research, University of Dhaka, Bangladesh

Abstract

Improving skills and values for employment has become a key focus of modern education, a trend also seen in Bangladesh. This shift is driven by high unemployment rates among college graduates, which reveal a significant gap between the skills graduates possess and those needed in the job market. In today's global economy, effective communication, specialized work skills, and interpersonal abilities are crucial for employability. There exists a notable disconnect between theoretical education and practical skill development, hindering graduates' readiness for employment. This study focuses specifically on Botany graduates from public universities in Bangladesh, examining the emphasis on employability skills in their curriculums and the perceptions of various stakeholders regarding this issue. Utilizing a multiple case study approach within a qualitative framework, the research selected four Botany curriculums from different universities for analysis. It was conducted in two phases: first, a review of curriculum content, followed by interviews and focus group discussions with stakeholders. The findings indicate significant variations in how botany curriculums of different public universities in Bangladesh prioritize employability skills and values, highlighting the need for harmonized curricula that better align with industry requirements. The study aims to inform curriculum reforms to enhance the development of employability skills, thereby bridging the gap between educational outcomes and employer expectations. The implications of this research extend to curriculum committees, faculty, students, university administrators, policymakers, and employers, offering valuable insights for preparing Botany graduates for a dynamic job market with reformed curriculums. Additionally, future researchers may benefit from a comparative understanding of employability skills across Botany curriculums, guiding further investigations in this area.

Teachers' understanding on science process skills of primary science teaching practice in Bangladesh: rural and urban perspectives

Dr. Rezina Ahmed
Associate Professor, Institute of Education and Research, University of Dhaka, Bangladesh,
Email: rezina@du.ac.bd

Dr. S M Hafizur Rahman
Professor, Institute of Education and Research, University of Dhaka, Bangladesh.

Abstract

Developing science process skills are one of the core aspects of science teaching-learning. However, teachers understanding of science process skills is a common query of effective science teaching practice. This study therefore explored teachers' understanding of the science process skills of primary science teaching practice in Bangladesh. A multiple case study approach was employed to collect data from purposively selected four primary science teachers from rural and urban areas of Bangladesh. Each teacher, his/her aligned students, and three concerned stakeholders (Assistant Upazila Education officers, instructors of Upazila Resource Center and Primary Teachers Training Institutes) are considered as a case. The relevant primary science textbooks (TB) and teacher's editions (TE) were also considered data sources. Lesson observation, semi-structured interviews, focus group discussions, and document analysis were used to gather data. Data for the rural and urban cases were analyzed through qualitative content analysis and thematic analysis. The findings reveal that in the primary science teaching practice of Bangladesh, teachers mostly have somewhat understanding of science process skills. The findings also indicate that concerned stakeholders have somewhat understanding of science process skills. However, teachers get professional support from the concerned stakeholders and curriculum documents (e.g., TE, TB). Besides adding value to the existing literature in science education, the findings are significant for the stakeholders (e.g., curriculum developers, policymakers, teacher trainers and researchers) from the Ministry of Primary and Mass Education (MoPME), Directorate of Primary Education (DPE), National Curriculum and Textbook Boards (NCTB), and National Academy for Primary Education (NAPE) to improve primary science teaching practices.

Educational Paradigm Shift: Linking School Conditions to Student Transition in Garissa Township Sub-County, Kenya.

Owuor Paul Felix paulfelixowour@gmail.com

Dr Aden Ali Abdi abdi.aadeen@gmail.com

Dr Robert Machyo machyorobert@gmail.com

Abstract

The most demanding phases for students are that of school transition, especially from primary school to junior school. This study was to examine the relationship between school conditions and student transition from primary school to junior school. Quantitative research design was used to investigated the association role of school conditions in student transition. The study targeted 336 teachers in 30 public primary schools within the Garissa Township sub-county. Census sampling technique was used to collect data, questionnaires were administered to collect data from teachers while face and content validity was used to measure the extent to which an instrument was intended to measure as Cronbach Alpha tests were done to analyse items for internal. The mean for school condition was 2.4(SD = 0.54) and the mean for student transition was 2.7(SD = .49). The relationship was positive, moderate in strength and statistically significant (r (244) = 0.172, p = 0.007 < 0.05). The positive monotonic association implies that as the quality of school conditions improves, there is a tendency for an increase in the rate of students transitioning from primary to junior school. The inferential statistics using Spearman's rank correlation was used to test bivariate correlation. The correlation coefficient of 0.172 indicates a positive direction, and its statistical significance (p = 0.007) The correlation is positive, it is important to note that the strength of this relationship is of a moderate magnitude. The findings provide evidence for a discernible and statistically significant association between the quality of school conditions and the process of student transition. The study provides valuable insights into student transitions from primary to junior school, emphasizing the significance of a positive school condition, aligned with Bronfenbrenner's Ecological Systems Theory. Acknowledging the weak correlation and advocating for a holistic approach, the research aligns with Brown et al. (2017), recognizing the multifaceted nature of transitions influenced by socio-economic factors and individual characteristics.

Empowering Education Through Innovation

Dr. Shivakumar G S
Principal, Kumadvathi College of Education, Shikaripura
Email: drshivakumargs@gmail.com

Abstract

In the 21st century, education is undergoing a rapid transformation, driven by innovation and technological advancements. "Empowering Education through Innovation" explores the pivotal role that creative solutions, digital tools, and new methodologies play in reshaping learning environments. This concept emphasizes the need to move beyond traditional approaches to make education more accessible, inclusive, and impactful.

The integration of technologies like artificial intelligence, e-learning platforms, and virtual classrooms has revolutionized how students learn and educators teach. These innovations enable personalized learning experiences, break down geographical and socio-economic barriers, and prepare students for a dynamic, technology-driven world. Gamification, blended learning, and project-based education further enhance student engagement and foster critical thinking and problem-solving skills.

Government policies, public-private partnerships, and a focus on teacher training are essential to scaling these innovations and ensuring they benefit a broader audience. As we look to the future, trends like virtual and augmented reality, blockchain for certifications, and lifelong learning models will continue to redefine education. Ultimately, empowering education through innovation fosters a generation of learners equipped to thrive in an evolving global landscape.

The abstract highlights the importance of embracing innovation to ensure that education remains a powerful tool for personal growth, societal progress, and global development.

Education in 2050: A Vision for the Future

Dr. Shivakumar G S
Principal, Kumadvathi College of Education, Shikaripura
Email: drshivakumargs@gmail.com

Abstract

By 2050, education is expected to undergo a dramatic transformation, driven by technological advancements, data analytics, and a deeper understanding of how humans learn. This vision of the future sees the integration of artificial intelligence (AI), virtual and augmented reality (VR/AR), and neuroscience into daily learning processes, enabling highly personalized and adaptive education experiences. AI tutors and data-driven insights will allow educators to customize lessons to suit each student's learning style, pace, and interests, maximizing student engagement and outcomes.

In addition, schools of the future will likely be less confined to physical spaces. Virtual classrooms, powered by immersive technologies, will enable global, borderless learning where students from different parts of the world can collaborate in real time. Traditional curricula will give way to interdisciplinary and project-based learning, equipping students with critical thinking, problem-solving, and creativity skills needed to thrive in an ever-evolving, technology-driven world.

Education in 2050 will also place greater emphasis on inclusivity and equity. Global online platforms and digital resources will help bridge educational gaps, providing quality learning opportunities to underserved communities. In this vision of the future, education evolves into a lifelong, borderless journey, tailored to each individual and supported by cutting-edge technology, ensuring that no one is left behind.

Study of Values of Secondary School Students in Relation to Modernization

Dr. Devaraja Y

Assistant Professor. Kumadvathi Colldge of Education, Shikaripura,
Email: ydevaraja@gmail.com

Abstract

The future of any nation depends on its children. Values play an important role in shaping the character and personality of the children. The present study attempts to study the values of secondary school students in relation to modernization. The main purpose of the study is to compare the values of secondary school boys and girls, rural and urban students and government and non-government secondary school students. In this study normative survey method was employed. All secondary school students of Shikaripura taluk constituted the population of the study. Random sampling technique was used to select a total number of 320 secondary school students from the government and non-government secondary schools of Shikaripura taluk. Mean, S.D., 't' test were used for the statistical analysis. The findings revealed that all the secondary school students had average level of values. They preferred social values most while religious value was least preferred by the students. Secondary school students of rural and urban area were found to differ significantly in the hedonistic, family prestige and health values of government and non-government secondary school students. Social, family prestige and health values of the students while the modernization did not put any significant influence on the values of the students.

Education, Technology and Peace – Promoting World Peace

Dr. Devaraja Y
Assistant Professor, Kumadvathi Colldge of Education, Shikaripura,
Email: ydevaraja@gmail.com

Abstract

Technology in itself has a very broad meaning. From wheel to the latest launched satellite, all comes under the development of technology for the peace of world. It has tremendous power to revolutionize the whole world and making it peaceful to live in. It has made our lives comfortable and easier in one or the other way by integrating us nationally and internationally. In today's scenario, our lives have become so complicated that we have to take its help in making our lives harmonious. It has wide application in developing peace worldwide. So, it is the duty of every single citizen of the nation to use it in the best possible ways for the betterment of human race. Though, we cannot deny the multiple harms of using technology but still we can try to minimise its affects and can use in the best possible ways for promoting peace. We have discussed 'Role of Technology in promoting World peace'. Instead of using Technology for violence, it should be used to promote peace. In this paper it has been discussed that what are the different areas where we can use technology for developing peace? What are the different ways that should be opted for promoting peace through it. ICT acts as an important tool to achieve the aim of developing harmony among individuals as well as with the society.. ICT can be used for identifying various problems related to environment through early warning systems, promoting their peaceful solution, supporting humanitarian actions, including protection of beings and assisting post conflict peace building and reconstruction. This paper is a comprehensive study of the crucial role of technology in developing and promoting peace.

A Comparative Study on Reading Habits of Underachievers in Academic Achievement of Secondary School Students

Dr. Veerendra Kumar Wali S.
Assistant Professor, Kumadvathi College of Education, Shikaripura. Shivamogga, Karnataka,
Email: veerendrakumarwalis@gmail.com

Abstract

"Knowledge Grows on the Bookshelf of Patience."
Knowledge of various writing styles and passages is essential for developing a better understanding of developing language passages. This will undoubtedly save you time and help you score

well in the most important area of most examinations' Verbal Ability section. The many writing styles are distinct from one another. Those who read more books, have more chances of mental development and better opportunities of success.

Hence, this paper is an attempt to find out relationship between underachievement's of students' reading habits and their academic performance in Secondary School Students. The questionnaire investigated students' reading habit and their attitudes towards reading. Students' academic performances were recorded through the transcripts of their examination in the previous semester. The researchers concluded that students do not read books frequently and Girls students take more interest in reading books than boy students. It is recommended that teachers and parents should create a conducive environment for students to read more and more books for effective learning. Students should also make library their first point of call to get updated from time to time for development of reading habits. Adequate and updated books, journals, newspaper must be available in the libraries, so that students could be attracted for more reading.

Leadership Behaviour among Student Teachers (B.Ed. Trainees)

Dr. Yadukumar M,
Assistant Professor, Kumadvathi College of Education, Shikariura,
Email: yadukumarm@gmail.com

Abstract

Education is a noble calling that entails both challenges and responsibilities. One of the main aims of education is to produce good leaders. Strong accountable leadership is always a hallmark of successful individuals. It is a known fact that, the development of a society depends on its directive leaders. A leader is one who guides, organizes, directs and co-ordinates the society. Leadership is the ability to persuade others to seek defined objectives enthusiastically.

Adequacy of leadership is very material for the students of higher education. Because, all B.Ed. trainees need leadership qualities and the related skills are needed virtually in all areas. It is the human factor, which binds a group together and motivates it towards the goals. To be effective leaders, they must bring the core principles of quality leadership to their decision making and interaction with others. The emotional component of leadership requires the ability to perceive emotions, facilitate emotions in thought and understand and manage emotions. Leaders possessing these abilities are considered emotionally intelligence. Because intelligently governed emotion play a significant role in directing and shaping one's leadership behaviour and personality.

The B.Ed. trainees with ample leadership behaviour can lead anything successfully. The present scenario necessitates the effective intelligent leaders. Being very much inspired by the above discussion, the investigator has prepared her mind to study the leadership behaviour of B.Ed. trainees.

Therefore, the primary goal of this study is to assess the leadership qualities of Student Teachers (B.Ed. Trainees). The secondary goal is to aid in the development of programs that promote leadership quality among Student Teachers.

The Influence of Lifestyle on Academic Performance among Student Teachers

Dr. Yadukumar M,
Assistant Professor, Kumadvathi College of Education, Shikariura,
Email: yadukumarm@gmail.com

Abstract

A healthy lifestyle, as defined by the World Health Organization, is a manner of living that reduces the likelihood of severe illness or early death and offers more than just disease prevention. It promotes the overall well-being of the individual including their physical, mental, and social health. Adopting a healthy lifestyle not only benefits the individual but also provides a positive example to those around them, such as family environment and professional environment.

The lifestyle factors of students have a significant influence on their academic performance. For example, a lack of physical activity and unhealthy eating habits negatively affect their academic performance. Sleep also plays a principal role in a healthy lifestyle. High quality sleep leads to improved cognitive processing as a person gets healthier, which leads to excellent academic performance. On the other hand, a lack of sleep is associated with higher anxiety, depression, and stress. Conversely, participation in healthy habits improves their academic performance and reduces absenteeism. Therefore, improving positive habits of students can benefit their academic outcomes.

Numerous other factors also impact students' academic success, including their motivation, physical well-being, and emotional state. In particular, elevated stress levels experienced by Student Teachers can have adverse effects on their cognitive abilities and learning, resulting in lower academic performance. However, including physical activity in Student Teachers routines yields several advantages. It improves cognitive function, enhances learning abilities, boosts self-perception, increases arousal, reduces boredom, alleviates stress, stabilizes moods, promotes better sleep, and enhances attention span and concentration.

Therefore, the primary goal of this study is to assess the impact of lifestyle factors, such as physical activity, sleep behaviour, dietary habits, and anxiety, on the academic performance of Student Teachers (B.Ed. Trainees). The secondary goal is to aid in the development of programs that promote healthier lifestyles among Student Teachers, ultimately improving their academic outcomes and overall well-being.

Innovative Educational Frameworks for Future Skills and Competencies

Dr. Ravi H

Assistant Professor, Kumadvathi College of Education, Shikaripura,
Email: ravikumarh.06@gmail.com

Abstract

In today's rapidly growing world, the traditional standards of education face unprecedented challenges in adequately preparing individuals for the complexities of the future. The landscape of work and society is undergoing profound conversions driven by technological advancements, globalization, and socio-economic shifts, thereby necessitating a fresh perspective on the skills and competencies required by the workforce. It is within this active context that the concept of "innovative educational frameworks for future skills and competencies" develops as a pivotal area of consideration and development.

This article endeavours to delve into and showcase pioneering educational methodologies explicitly tailored to equip learners with the future skills and competencies indispensable for thriving in the 21st century and beyond. Recognizing that the mere transmission of information falls short, we advocate for an education system that fosters critical thinking, creativity, adaptability, collaboration, and above all, a lifelong learning mind-set. These "future skills" are not only imperative for professional success but also for active citizenship and personal fulfilment amidst an increasingly intricate world. Through an amalgamation of diverse perspectives and illuminative case studies, this article seeks to dissect how educators, policymakers, and stakeholders are reconceptualising education to meet the future's demands. From immersive project-based learning and competency-driven education to innovative interdisciplinary approaches and the integration of cutting-edge technologies, each concept will offer insights into promising strategies and frameworks poised to prepare students for the challenges and prospects of tomorrow. Additionally, this article underscores the significance of addressing equity, diversity, and inclusion within educational contexts. Confirming universal access to high-quality education, regardless of background or circumstance, is not only a moral imperative but also a cornerstone for nurturing a fairer and more successful society.

Innovative Teaching Methodologies and Practices for School Education in the Indian Scenario

Dr. Ravi H
Assistant Professor, Kumadvathi College of Education, Shikaripura,
Email: ravikumarh.06@gmail.com

Abstract

In a rapidly changing world, the methods of teaching are evolving alongside advancements in technology and shifts in societal expectations. The Indian education system, rich in tradition and diversity, faces the dual challenge of maintaining its cultural heritage while embracing innovation. As educators strive to engage students more effectively, a focus on innovative practices and methodologies becomes paramount. In this article, we will explore the historical of teaching practices in India, the diverse methodologies employed, the challenges faced by educators, and innovative approaches that are transforming classrooms. And various fascinating approaches that have the potential to transform school education in India.

Innovative teaching practices and methodologies have the power to rejuvenate the Indian education system. By embracing strategies such as experiential learning, flipped classrooms, technology integration, community collaboration, and inquiry-based learning, educators can create an environment that inspires students. From experiential learning to the integration of technology, we will uncover methods that not only enhance academic performance but also nurture holistic development.

Challenges and Opportunities in Digital Education

Dr. Vani Nayaki D.C,
Assistant Professor, Kumadvathi College of Education, Shikaripura,
Email: vaninayaki@gmail.com

Abstract

Education is a purposeful activity directed at achieving certain aims, such as transmitting knowledge or fostering skills and character traits. These aims may include the development of understanding, rationality, kindness, and honesty. Various researchers emphasize the role of critical thinking in order to distinguish education from indoctrination. Some theorists require that education results in an improvement of the student while others prefer a value-neutral definition of the term. In a slightly different sense, education may also refer, not to the process, but to the product of this process:

the mental states and dispositions possessed by educated people. Digital Education refers to the integration of technology with educational practices to enhance teaching and learning outcomes. In the 21st Century, a majority of individuals sue the internet regularly to increase their knowledge and to foster general awareness in this era of globalization. Due to the recent Covid-19 pandemic people and students are facing problems in their study or gaining access to high quality knowledge. We face the many challenges in the field of Education through technology like: Legacy processes and Manual handling. Many businesses still rely on traditional, paper-based processes for document management and complexity of Document formats. And data quality and accuracy, integration with Existing systems and Security and Compliance.

Curriculum Approaches

Dr. Vani Nayaki D C
Assistant Professor, Kumadvathi College of Education, Shikaripura.
Email: vaninayaki@gmail.com

Abstract

Education is a purposeful activity directed at achieving certain aims, such as transmitting <u>knowledge</u> or fostering skills and character traits. These aims may include the development of understanding, rationality, kindness, and honesty. Various researchers emphasize the role of critical thinking in order to distinguish education from indoctrination. Some theorists require that education results in an improvement of the student while others prefer a value-neutral definition of the term. In a slightly different sense, education may also refer, not to the process, but to the product of this process: the mental states and dispositions possessed by educated people. Education originated as the transmission of cultural heritage from one generation to the next. Today, educational goals increasingly encompass new ideas such as the liberation of learners, skills needed for modern society, empathy, and complex vocational skills. The path or ways of systematic Organization of content and learning experiences based on educational objectives is called as Approaches of Curriculum Organization. Once we understood the basic meaning of curriculum through varied definitions proposed by educationists, it is apt to understand the design of curriculum. it is essential to know the basic elements and their relationships. In any given curriculum, it is important to identify basic elements which are necessary. There is no consensus on these elements. However here identified the following 3 elements. Like learning experiences, skills and Values and ideas.

The Importance of Physical Education and its Effect on Academic Performance

Ravikumar N.G.

Physical Education Director, Kumadvathi College of Education, Shikaripur, Shivamogga, (Karnataka) Email: ravikumarng79@gmail.com

Abstract

Health is a vital moderating factor in a child's ability to learn. The idea that healthy children learn better is empirically supported and well accepted (Basch, 2010). Many factors influence the academic performance of a child. In adults, brain health, representing absence of disease and optimal structure and function, is measured in terms of quality of life and effective functioning of activities in daily living. In children, brain health is measured in terms of successful development of attention, on-task behavior, memory and academic performance in an educational setting. Physical activity and fitness plays a vital role in developing the brain during childhood. Children respond faster and with greater accuracy to a variety of cognitive tasks after participating in a session of physical activity. Participating in moderate physical activity is found to increase neural and behavioral concomitants associated with the allocation of attention to a specific cognitive task. In some experimental study, children who participated in 30 minutes of aerobic physical activity outperformed those children who watched television for the same amount of time. Physical activity which is generally used as a break from academic learning time, post engagement effects of it includes better attention, increased on-task behaviours and improved academic performance

A Comparative Study of the Effect of Pranayama Exercises and Endurance Exercises on Heart & Lungs Capacity

Ravikumar N.G.
Physical Education Director, Kumadvathi College of Education
Shikaripur, Shivamogga District, Karnataka, E-Mail : ravikumarng79@gmail.com

Abstract

Pranayama is a Sanskrit word which consists of prana and ayama. Prana means self-energizing life forces and ayama means extension. Pranayama may be defined as expansion and control of prana through various yogic techniques. In a simple way, we can say that pranayama is a combination of systematic exhalation and inhalation. Increasing awareness to lifestyle disease has led to more participation of people in taking up various forms of Pranayama and exercise to avail more health benefits. The ability to perform physical exercise is related to cardiovascular systems capacity to supply oxygen to muscles and pulmonary systems ability to clear carbon di oxide from blood via lungs. The purpose of this study is not only to assess the beneficial effects of pranayama and endurance exercises but to compare the improvements in the heart & lung functions among these two modalities of exercises. Researcher Randomly selected men having age group 30 to 40 years having no previous history of Pranayama & endurance exercises, from Shivamogga City. N= 150 These sample are Randomly distributed in to 3 groups, each group of 50. Group-A= 50+Group-B= 50+Group-C= 50. Both pranayama and endurance exercise play an important role in improving the heart and pulmonary functions but effects were more pronounced with pranayama.

Digital Libraries in India: A Review

Vishwanatha G
Librarian. Kumadvathi College of Education, Shikaripura
E-mail: vishwanathg79@gmail.com

Abstract

During the past recent years, there has been tremendous development reaming the concept of digital libraries-a knowledge base that can be stored and retrieved through on-line networks. Digital libraries are the most complex form of information systems that support digital document preservation, distributed database management, hypertext, filtering, information retrieval and selective dissemination of information. This has really overcome geographical barrier offering wide range of academic, research and cultural resources with multimedia effects which can be accessed around the world over the distributed networks. A Digital library is a special library with a collection of digital objects that can include text, visual material, audio material, video material, stored as electronic media formats (as opposed to print, or other media.), along with means for organizing, storing, and retrieving the files and media contained in the library collection

A Study of Interest in Science in Relation to Academic Achievement of Secondary School Students in Science

Prasannakumar S
Research Scholar**,** Karnatak University, Dharwad
Email: prasannakumarsaparegn@gmail.com

Abstract

This study gives information about how Interest in science influence students' academic achievement. Interest in science is a students' driving force motivating towards acquiring knowledge of scientific concepts, facts, to do experiment, verify results and to get good grades in academic achievement of secondary school. Interest are of two types, one situational interest and other individual interest in this article we study both of the types, their examples and way of developing these types of interest to enhance students' academic achievement. Finally we can see conclusion and educational implication of the study.

Classroom Environment and Teacher Education in the 21st Century

Geena Koshy
Assistant Professor, Mar Baselios College of Education, Wayanad, Kerala
Email: geenaofficial12357@gmail.com

Abstract

The education of 'Z' generation demands a balance of updated knowledge and 21st -century skills. The demographic specialty of our country is that it is developing as a country with majority of people in the working age group. Highly talented and dedicated human resource is needed to lead our nation from a developing to a developed global power. For this, advanced teaching methodologies, enjoyable learning, and innovative evaluation strategies are needed. In this context, the environment of the classroom that supports teaching, learning and evaluation is very crucial. The concept of a classroom environment has already undergone significant transformations in the past decade in schools and colleges. This paper identifies the various issues of teaching, learning and evaluation related to classroom situations in higher educational sector, especially in teacher educational institutions, where the classrooms must be much more than merely functional. This paper makes an in-depth analysis of various strategies to improve the present classroom environment in the context of NEP 2020. Critical pedagogy and novel developments such as flipped classrooms are focused and discussed.

Reimagining Education: The Role of VR and AR

Nitha S.V.
Research Scholar, Regional Institute of Education (NCERT, Mysore)
Gmail: nsv2007@gmail.com

Prof. Ramadas V
Professor, Regional Institute of Education (NCERT, Mysore) Gmail: vrdash@gmail.com

Abstract

By enabling immersive and dynamic learning environments, virtual and augmented reality (VR/AR) has the potential to completely transform the educational landscape. This article explores how these technologies can enhance student motivation, improve learning outcomes, and create more dynamic teaching methods. Learning can be made more engaging by simulating worlds in virtual reality

(VR) where students can conduct experiments, study historical events, or navigate challenging terrain. Augmented Reality (AR) superimposes digital data on the physical world, improving comprehension of intangible ideas and promoting experiential learning. These technologies make abstract concepts accessible and engaging, which increases student motivation and improves learning results. While AR can bring textbook diagrams to life, virtual reality (VR) can take students to remote landscapes or historical civilizations in courses like geography and history. VR simulations offer authentic practice environments for professional training, improving skills and readiness. There are, however, drawbacks, such as the expensive price of VR gear and content creation and worries about a decline in social contact. Despite these obstacles, VR and AR have the potential to drastically improve and alter educational experiences with careful application and investment.

Effect of Constructivists-Based Teaching on Science Attitude of Students at Secondary School Level of Belthangady Taluk

Vidhyashree P
Research Scholar, Institute of Education, Srinivas University, Mangalore, India.
Email: shree11vidya@gmail.com

Abstract

The study dealt on the effectiveness of Constructivists based teaching on the student's attitude towards science. This approach has six stages of learning. The present study is experimental study post-test equivalent group design. All students of Beltangady taluk were taken as a population of the study. Randomly selected 70 students were samples of the study. Science Attitude Scale, constructed by Mrs. Avinash Grewal. Data was collected and analysed using statistical techniques, 't' at 0.05 level of significance. The result of the study revealed that Constructivists based teaching had the significant effect in developing Science Attitude among Secondary School Students.

Role of Social and Emotional Learning among Higher Primary School Students

Poornima Shamarao Ramateerth
Research Scholar, Department of Education and Research Studies. Gulbarga University, Kalaburgi.
Gmail: poornimasr544@gmail.com
Dr. Hoovinabhavi B L
Professor, & Research Guide, Department of Education and Research Studies. Gulbarga University, Kalaburgi. Gmail: hoovinbhavibl@gmail.com

Abstract

The present study aimed to investigate the effect of social and emotional learning among higher primary school students. The study consists of 156 students from Kalaburgi and Yadgir districts of

Karnataka state, divided equally into groups based on the school type and gender. The Social and Emotional Learning Scale (Coelho, Sousa, & Marchante, 2015) was used to measure SEL. Statistical analysis involved mean, standard deviation, and t-tests. Findings indicate significant differences in SEL between rural and urban students. Additionally, sociodemographic factors like school type, gender, and medium of instruction influence SEL among higher primary school students in these districts. The paper discusses implications and recommendations based on these results.

A Study on Awareness of Learning Games among Secondary School Students

Kiran Premkumar Malge

Research Scholar, Department of Education Rani Channamma University, Belagavi,
Email: kiranmalge82@gmail.com

Dr. Sushma R,

Assistant Professor, Department of Education, Rani Channamma University, Belagavi,
Email: sushmarcueducation@gmail.com

Abstract

Learning games is widespread among Secondary school students. The aim of this study is to know the Learning games of the Secondary school students. We used from a field method to collect the required data and complete the standard questionnaire. The study was based on Survey. The statistical population was 118 students of the Secondary school students in the 2024-2025 academic year. One hundred eighteen students were selected. According to the results, the necessity of using games in Secondary school students. The results shows that most of the students in Secondary school using different learning games hence, the study concludes that learning games are very important and need of the hour.

Effect of Constructivists-Based Teaching on Science Attitude of Students at Secondary School Level of Belthangady Taluk

Vidhyashree P

Research Scholar, Institute of Education, Srinivas University, Mangalore, India.
Email: shree11vidya@gmail.com

Abstract

The study dealt on the effectiveness of Constructivists based teaching on the student's attitude towards science. This approach has six stages of learning. The present study is experimental study post-test equivalent group design. All students of Beltangady taluk were taken as a population of the study. Randomly selected 70 students were samples of the study. Science Attitude Scale, constructed by Mrs.

Avinash Grewal. Data was collected and analysed using statistical techniques, 't' at 0.05 level of significance. The result of the study revealed that Constructivists based teaching had the significant effect in developing Science Attitude among Secondary School Students.

Building Future-Ready Minds: Key Skills and Competencies for 21st-Century Education

Dr. Nagaratna S
Guest Faculty, Smt.Veeramma Gangasiri Degree College for Women, Kalabuargi,
Email: nagaratnashivakumar@gmail.com

Abstract

The educational landscape is evolving to meet the needs of future learners and workers in a world shaped by rapid technological advancement, globalization, and societal shifts. Influential figures like Dr. A.P.J. Abdul Kalam and Dr. K. Kasturirangan have advocated for a holistic, future-oriented approach to education. The shift from traditional to modern practices reflects the changing demands of industries, focusing on flexibility, lifelong learning, and human-centered skills.

Key competencies for 21st-century education include digital literacy, technological competence, critical thinking, and problem-solving, enabling students to thrive in a tech-driven world and address complex challenges. Social and emotional learning (SEL) promotes emotional intelligence and personal development, while adaptability and resilience equip learners for dynamic environments. STEM skills are essential for innovation, and lifelong learning fosters continuous growth. Emphasizing mental health ensures balanced development, and research and innovation drive personalized learning, helping bridge educational disparities.

In conclusion, education in the 21st century must extend beyond academics, preparing students with diverse skills to navigate an uncertain, evolving world, and empowering them to contribute meaningfully to society.

Construction and Standardization of Academic Self-Indiscipline Scale (ASIS) among Teacher Education Students

Santosh Kumar. M J
Research Scholar, Department of Education, Kuvempu University, Shankaraghatta, Shivamogga,
Karnataka, India, Email: santoshkumarmj29@gmail.com
Geetha. C
Professor, Department of Education, Kuvempu University, Shankaraghatta, Shivamogga, Karnataka,
India, Email: geetha.edu@gmail.com

Abstract

Academic self-indiscipline, characterized by poor time management and ineffective study habits, is a significant barrier to student success. This study aims to develop and validate the Academic Self-Indiscipline Scale (ASIS) to measure these challenges specifically among teacher education students. The ASIS Scale assesses two key dimensions: management skills, which include task prioritization and time allocation, and study habits, reflecting consistent and effective learning strategies. The scale was constructed and refined through rigorous processes, including expert review, pilot testing, and item analysis. Reliability was established using test-retest, split-half, and Cronbach's alpha methods, with results of 0.889 for management skills, 0.818 for study habits, and an overall reliability coefficient of 0.917. Content and item validity were confirmed through expert evaluation and statistical analysis. The final scale comprises 20 items, with a scoring system ranging from 20 to 80. This study highlights the importance of addressing academic self-discipline to enhance academic performance and preparedness for the teaching profession. The ASIS Scale provides a robust tool for identifying at-risk students and informing targeted interventions.

The Use of AI Software in Teaching: Transforming Education

Dr. Kowshik M.C
Assistant. Professor, B.E.A College of Education, Davanagere, Karnataka.
E-mail: koushikmc1976@gmail.com

Abstract

Through the improvement of teaching strategies, personalization of learning, and efficiency in the classroom, artificial intelligence (AI) is transforming the field of education. The transformational potential of AI in education is discussed in this article, which focuses on key issues including virtual tutors, automated exams, and individualized learning. AI software can promote inclusivity by offering accessible learning solutions, optimize instructional time by automating repetitive chores, and customize educational content to meet the needs of specific students. AI-powered resources like Quizlet, Duolingo, and Khanmigo are prime examples of how gamification, real-time feedback, and adaptive learning pathways are changing education. Additionally, by utilizing immersive technologies like virtual reality (VR) and augmented reality (AR), AI promotes increased student engagement. Notwithstanding the advantages, moral issues pertaining to justice, accessibility, and teacher readiness need to be considered. AI's application in education has enormous potential to improve learning outcomes and build a more diverse, individualized, and data-driven learning environment as it develops.

The Role of Artificial Intelligence in Teaching Sports, Physical, and Health Education

Chandregowda.S
Physical Education Director., B.E.A College of Education, Davanagere, Karnataka
E-mail: chandregowdakg@gmail.com

Abstract

Artificial Intelligence (AI) is revolutionizing sports, physical, and health education by enhancing personalization, student engagement, and real-time feedback. This paper explores the integration of AI technologies such as machine learning, data analytics, and virtual reality to improve performance analysis, create tailored training programs, and offer adaptive learning experiences in physical and health education. AI also assists in injury prevention, rehabilitation, and coaching, while addressing accessibility for diverse learners. Despite its benefits, challenges such as data privacy, costs, and the need for teacher training must be managed for effective implementation. AI's role in reshaping education is both promising and transformative.

Effectiveness of Teacher Education in Mentorship and Teacher Leadership

Dr. Haleshappa T
Assistant Professor, M.M College of Education, Davangere
E-mail: haleshmmclg@gmail.com

Abstract

This paper describes the views of Effectiveness of Teacher education in teacher leadership and mentorship, also this paper reports the role of teacher education to design to gain a better understanding of the mentoring experience. Mentoring is a vitally important mechanism to benefit and train the next generation of knowledge creators and disseminators. Mentoring, as one of the formal teacher leadership roles, creates a space for teachers to display their leadership potential as it indirectly brings value to the school community. The purpose of these qualitative views is to examine mentor teachers' perceptions whether they transfer their evolving mentoring skills into other leadership practices. Mentoring is a powerful way to develop teacher leadership, which is the ability to influence and improve teaching and learning beyond one's own classroom. Effective mentoring can help teachers grow professionally, collaborate with peers, and take on leader. The various reasons that teacher mentoring within schools is beneficial for schools, teachers, and students. Mentoring within schools promotes teacher retention and consistency among educators. Mentoring programs not only increase job satisfaction and help teachers to emerge as leaders within their schools, but also have a positive effect on student achievement and engagement. Mentoring allows people to learn from one another and facilitates the transmission of knowledge. Mentoring, rather than developing specific academic abilities or information, focuses on building confidence and relationships, developing resilience and character, and raising expectations.

Technological Integration in Teaching

Dr. P. B. Kavyakishore

Assistant Professor, P.G. Dept. of Education, R.V Teachers College (IASE)
Bengaluru, Email: drkk.iase@gmail.com

Abstract

Teachers at all levels of education, from preschool to college-level courses, might use a wide range of technological tools to teach content and build skills. This process, called technological integration, can transform students' learning experiences and provide a range of benefits. Learning about technological integration can help an educator create lesson plans that use digital tools effectively to meet curriculum goals. In this article, we define technological integration, explore the four levels of technology integration and several frameworks for this process, provide benefits of this practice and list common digital tools you can use in your classroom.

Importance of Future Skills and Competencies in Education

Annapurna A
Research scholar, Karnataka State Open University, Mukthagangothri,
Mysuru. Email: annapurnaa145@gmail.com

Dr. N. Lakshmi
Professor & Dean Academic, Karnataka State Open University, Mukthagangothri,
Mysuru, Email: shaibhat@yahoo.co.in

Abstract

At present world is transforming rapidly. Each individual has to imbibe certain skills and competencies to habitat themselves in the transforming world. Education connects an individual to the fast-evolving world through its promotion of skills and competencies. Skills development is at the center changes happening in educational trends such as digitalization, Artificial Intelligence, climate change, which are changing the nature of education and skills demand. These evolving trends will redefine the paradigms of education systems globally. Consequently, skills and competencies development must proactively adapt to fast transformation posed by the changing systems. The traditional days are no longer useful with degree and specialization. One needs to imbibe skills and competencies which help one to survive in the future transforming world. In this article the significance of future skills and competencies in education discussed in detail.

The Effect of Stress on the Academic Achievement of Prospective Teachers

Dr. Shashikala M S

Assistant Professor, R V Teachers College (IASE), Bengaluru,
Email: shashikalamath@gmail.com

Abstract

This study investigates the effect of stress on the academic achievement of prospective teachers. Using Survey Method, data was collected from 80 participants through Purposive Sampling. The study utilized Students Stress Scale (SSS)Questionnaire to measure stress levels, and statistical tools like Percentage Analysis and t-test were applied to analyse the data. The results indicated that the overall stress level of prospective teachers is moderate. There is no significant differences were found in stress levels based on gender The study highlights the importance of incorporating stress management strategies, such as meditation and relaxation techniques, into teacher training programs to enhance academic success among future educators.

Advance Organizer Model, An Innovative Strategy in Developing Conceptual Structure in Biological Science – A Perspective

Dr. Janaki M.
Research Guide & Assistant Professor, Department of Studies in Education,
Karnataka State Open University, Mukthagangotri, Mysuru, E-mail: janakiksou@gmail.com

Ms. Rashmi N.
Research Scholar, RV Teachers College, IASE, Bengaluru,
E-mail: rashmirao0411@gmail.com

Abstract

The Advance Organizer Model, AOM, has been developed as an effective tool for pedagogy, especially in terms of biological science. This paper takes up the challenging prospective scope that AOM can have towards developing conceptual structure and enriching the student's grasp of concepts. The AOM gives it a formative shape which connects the existing information with the new piece of information and enhances meaningful learning and retention. This paper covers the theoretical underpinning of AOM, practical application of AOM in the education of biological science, and evidence about its effectiveness. It is in conclusion that AOM will ensure that students are taught with better understanding, develop critical thinking skills, and establish reasons to learn biology for life.

Blockchain in Educational Credentialing: Revolutionizing Trust and Transparency in Academic Records

Dr Nandini A
Assistant Professor, NMKRV college for women, Bangalore, Email:

Dr. Geetha C
Professor, P.G Department of Studies & Research in Education, Kuvempu University, Shankaraghatta, Email:

Abstract

Blockchain technology is revolutionizing educational credentialing by enhancing trust, transparency, and efficiency in academic records management. This paper presents key steps for successful blockchain implementation in educational institutions, including readiness assessment, stakeholder engagement, and defining clear objectives. It reveals the importance of selecting appropriate blockchain platforms and navigating complex regulatory frameworks, such as GDPR and FERPA for data protection. Furthermore, the paper highlights the need for robust identity management systems and clear intellectual property policies to safeguard the integrity of digital credentials.

Long-term sustainability strategies—encompassing financial planning, technical maintenance, and effective governance frameworks—are discussed to ensure the ongoing effectiveness of blockchain systems. By addressing these critical areas, this work serves as a comprehensive guide for educational institutions aiming to adopt blockchain technology. It aims to foster trust and transparency in credentialing processes, ultimately enhancing the educational experience for students, faculty, and administrators.

Through strategic planning and collaboration, blockchain credentialing is positioned as a pivotal advancement in the future of academic record management. This technology offers significant benefits for all stakeholders involved in the education ecosystem, facilitating secure and verifiable credentialing practices that can adapt to evolving educational needs.

Challenges and Opportunity in Teacher Education Under NPE-2020

Bhavani. N
Assistant Professor, NMKRV College For Women, Bangalore,
Email: bhavani.n82@gmail.com

Abstract

The National Education Policy (NEP) 2020, the first major education reform of the 21st century, seeks to address India's evolving developmental needs by restructuring the educational framework, with a strong emphasis on teachers as central to the reform process. This paper highlights the challenges and opportunities in teacher education under NEP 2020. Key challenges include modernizing outdated teacher training programs, improving practical exposure, and ensuring equitable access to quality education, especially in rural and remote areas. These challenges underscore the need for a more inclusive and robust teacher education system.

On the other hand, NEP 2020 presents numerous opportunities for innovation in teacher education. The policy advocates for the development of multidisciplinary, practice-based training, continuous professional development, and the integration of modern pedagogical tools. It seeks to professionalize teaching, enhancing the status of educators and placing them at the heart of societal progress. The focus on holistic and experiential learning enables teachers to foster critical thinking, creativity, and ethical values in students.

This paper emphasizes that with effective implementation, NEP 2020 can revolutionize teacher education, building an equitable, future-oriented system that aligns with global standards while preserving India's cultural heritage.

A Meta-Analysis on the Effect of Test Anxiety on the Academic Achievement

Dr. Manjula K. Swamy
Assistant Professor, RV Teachers College, Bengaluru,
Email: swamy.manjula@gmail.com

Abstract

Education is more concerned with academic achievement of students. Academic achievement refers to the extent or degree of mastery in certain areas of studies. Academic achievement refers to the knowledge accomplished or attained and skills developed by him/her in the school subjects, usually designed test scores or by marks assigned by teachers. It means the achievement of the students in the academic subjects such as languages, social science, general science, arithmetic etc. Academic achievement is a key mechanism through which adolescents learn about their talents, abilities and competencies which are an important part of developing career aspirations (Lent et al., 2000). There are various factors that affect the achievement of the students one such factor is the academic anxiety of the students.

Several studies have been conducted with respect to the effect of test anxiety on the academic achievement. The researcher has included the studies conducted from 2012 to till date. (2024) the studies showed that the test anxiety shows a negative impact on the academic achievement of the stu Academic anxiety is one of the factors that affect academic achievement of students

The main purpose of this study is to conduct a meta-analysis to provide quant Academic anxiety is one of the factors that affect academic achievement of students. quantative   analysis of the research findings on the effect of test anxiety on the academic achievement.

A Study the Impact of Emerging Technology on Academic Achievement of Students in Karnataka University Dharwad

Dr. Kumar Dasar
Assistant Master, S B High School Yaragatti, Belagavi,
Email: Kumardasarphd1@gmail.com

Abstract

The main aim of this study is to find out how technologies influence the academic performance of students in Karnataka University. The study used ex post facto research design using quantitative method for data collection. Findings from the analyzed data showed that emerging technologies are available for use in various departments of the university. For example, mobile phones (93.8%), internet (88.8%), laptops/desktops (86.8%), projectors (82.1%), electronic books (68.1%), tablets (62.2%) and online courses (50.4%) accounted for more than half of the respondents. Available and accessible to more people. Mobile phones, laptops/desktops, intelligent personal assistants (IPAs), projectors, e-books, internet and e-learning lab equipment are evenly distributed across departments and the rest are statistically not evenly distributed. In addition, the study found that there is a negative relationship between the extent to which respondents use emerging technologies and their academic performance. However, Internet use recorded a statistically significant association with a p-value of 0.040.

The Evolution of MOOCs: Transforming Learning in the Digital Era

Dr. Santhosh Kumar R
Assistant professor, M M College of Education, Davangere, Karnataka,
Email: smgsanthosh@gmail.com

Abstract

The evolution of Massive Open Online Courses (MOOCs) has significantly transformed the educational landscape, making learning more accessible and flexible for individuals worldwide. Emerging in the early 2010s, MOOCs democratized education by allowing participants from diverse backgrounds to enroll in high-quality courses from prestigious institutions at little to no cost. This article examines the advantages of MOOCs, including their accessibility, flexibility, and the ability to foster a global learning community. However, it also addresses challenges such as high dropout rates, limited personalization, and concerns regarding quality assurance. The integration of MOOCs into traditional education through blended learning models and the offering of micro-credentials has further enhanced their relevance. Looking ahead, the future of MOOCs appears promising, with trends indicating a shift toward personalized learning experiences, skills-based courses, and increased collaboration between educational institutions and industry leaders. By harnessing emerging technologies like artificial intelligence, virtual reality, and augmented reality, MOOCs can continue to innovate and provide valuable learning opportunities. Ultimately, embracing the potential of MOOCs will be crucial for fostering a more inclusive, skilled, and educated global society.

Cognizance of Education Psychology –An Effective Instrument for Teaching Special Children

Dr. C B Vikram
Assistant Professor, JSS Institute of Education, Sakleshpur, Hassan, Karnataka,
E-Mail: vikramcb1977@gmail.com

Abstract

Educational psychology is an attempt to approach a child with empathy as well as with knowledge about their emotional, cognitive, social and behavioral needs. The challenges that, children are facing today are unprecedented. The pandemic has disrupted their education, their social life and altered their perception of the world forever. At such a time, it is even more important to make space for their anxieties, fears and possible inability to focus single-mindedly on academics. In a nutshell, educational psychology is not just about how children are behaving or faring in academics but is focused on all-around development as they transition from child hood and adolescence. It teaches to understand that learning is retained in different ways and that instructional methods must address the social, emotional, and cognitive particularities of the Special children.

Child who has a disability or learning problem that makes it harder for them to learn or do other activities than other children their age. Children with special needs may have difficulty with schoolwork, communication, or behaviour. Educational psychology is a constantly evolving field and researchers are busy exploring how to empower children with these special needs and so that together they can get past the factors that inhibit learning. It helps to identify children with special needs, tackle classroom problems, skills and interest in teaching, effective methods of teaching, the influence of heredity and environment on the child, the mental health of the child, the procedure of curriculum-making, guidance and counseling, assessment and evaluation. The present paper will describe the cognizance of Education Psychology is a prime instrument to become an effective classroom teacher in solving the problems of special children in the present education system.

Digital Literacy for Teacher Educators

Harini. P
Student Teacher, 3rd Semester, Master of Education, RV Teachers College, Bengaluru, Karnataka,
Email: harinip83@gmail.com

Abstract

In the digital age, enhancing digital literacy among teacher educators is essential for preparing future teachers to navigate and integrate technology effectively in their classrooms. This presentation examines the critical components of digital literacy, including technical skills, information evaluation, communication, collaboration, and content creation. We discuss current trends in educational technology and their implications for teaching practices, emphasizing the need for a framework such as TPACK (Technological Pedagogical Content Knowledge) to guide curriculum design.

Key strategies for developing digital literacy include ongoing professional development, peer collaboration, and experiential learning opportunities. We also address challenges such as resistance to change, resource constraints, and the rapid evolution of technology, highlighting the importance of adaptive teaching practices. Best practices from successful institutions illustrate how digital literacy can be effectively integrated into teacher education programs.

This presentation advocates for a proactive approach to digital literacy, empowering teacher educators to cultivate the skills necessary for fostering a technology-rich learning environment. By embracing these competencies, we can ensure that future educators are well-equipped to engage and inspire their students in an increasingly digital world.

Effectiveness of the Project-Based Learning Approach as a Way to Active Participation of Students in Learning

Puneetha V N
Student Teacher, 3rd Semester, Master of Education, RV Teachers College, Bengaluru, Karnataka,
Email: punithavn1372@gmail.com

Abstract

Project-Based Learning (PBL) is a transformative method of learning from teacher centered approach to student centered approach. It emphasizes the learning through active participation of students in the classroom. In this method, students work in groups through various projects which poster them to think critically, creatively and collaboratively. Project- based learning leads an individual not only mastery the subject but also leads to explore different skills like problem solving skills, communication skills, time management skills…etc. Research shows that PBL can lead to improved retention of information and greater student motivation. It is a powerful tool in modern education, where students get hands on experience of learning. Educator can fulfill the needs of 21st century students through this method.

Yoga in Education

Sreedev T E
Student Teacher, 3rd Semester, Master of Education, RV Teachers College, Bengaluru, Karnataka,
Email: sreeedevtekuttiattoor@gmail.com

Abstract

Yoga Asanas, Pranayama, Meditation, Mudras etc. should be made a part of daily life. Studies have shown that all physical and mental diseases of a person can be eradicated through this Sadhana.
The aim of this paper is to explain the relevance of yoga in education. Making yoga a part of the curriculum helps to minimize stress in children. It paves the way for students' success in life. Apart from an exercise, Yoga is also practiced as a competitive sport in the world today. Yoga competition is in various stages from school level to international level. By teaching Yoga along with other subjects in schools, it is possible to achieve better progress in the field of education and society.

Digital Pedagogy: Transforming Teaching and Learning in the 21st Century

Dr. Sarita Anand
Assistant Professor, Department of Education, Vinaya Bhavana, Visva-Bharati,
Email: sarita.anand@visva-bharati.ac.in

Shubha Sarkar
Junior Research Fellow, Department of Education, Vinaya Bhavana, Visva-Bharati
Email: shubhasarkar52@gmail.com

Abstract

Background: Digital pedagogy is transforming the present educational scenario by combining teaching-learning and technology to create engaging, effective, and accessible educational experiences. It involves using digital tools, technologies, and methods to support teaching and learning, enhancing student outcomes, and fostering innovative educational practices. The present research paper tries to explore the digital pedagogy in present classroom teaching-learning context. Literature review: An exhaustive literature review was done to identify the research problem in this study.

Research Question: How does digital pedagogy effect on student learning outcomes and teacher effectiveness in an educational setting? Methodology: This mixed-methods study combines survey, interview, and content analysis to investigate digital pedagogy's effect on:

1. Student learning outcomes (academic achievement, motivation).

2. Teacher effectiveness (instructional design, professional development).

Sample: 50 teachers and 150 students from higher education institutions of West Bengal.

Data Analysis: Quantitative data will be analyzed using descriptive and inferential statistics. Qualitative data will be coded, themed, and content analysis will be done.

Significance: This study may contribute to the understanding of digital pedagogy's potential to revolutionize present education. Findings will inform educators, policymakers, and researchers on effective strategies for integrating digital pedagogy in teaching-learning process.

Innovative Teaching Methods in the Classroom

Smt. Malakshmi
Assistant Professor in Education, Mandavya College of Education Mandya, Karnataka,
Email ID: malamahalakshmi884@gmail.com

Abstract

Advance pedagogy is the way to improve teaching and learning performance. Dissimilar innovative teaching methods are now in use across the world. Hybrid teaching includes e-learning in adding together to the face-to-face teaching. Use of elegant gadgets for dissimilar tasks like teaching, designing question papers, evaluation of student, feedback and research methodology is discussed. The application of innovative teaching and learning methods is critical if we are to inspire and engender a strength of learning as well as enthusiasm on the part of students, the role of education is to make certain that while academic staffs do teach, what is taught should also be understandable to students emanating from culturally and linguistically varied backgrounds and that they rapidly become familiar with the predictable standards. Lecturers should thus be appropriate themselves to utilizing innovative methods so that the students' learning process is as free-flowing as probable and that the methodology they adopt is favorable to learning. The major purpose of this paper aims to understand the different innovative teaching methods applying in the classroom.

Digital Education: Opportunities and Challenges

Smt. Gayathri K. J.
Assistant Professor, Mandavya College of Education, Mandya, Karnataka, India,

Abstract

National Education Policy 2020 documented the significance of digital education in given that quality education for all. Education is the procedure of facilitating learning, attainment of knowledge, skills, principles, attitude, habits etc. to give in socio-economic enlargement of nation. Digital education is a multifaceted multidimensional topic which uses digital technology and tools in teaching and learning procedure. Digital education provides a lot of opportunities to both teachers as well to their students. Students as well as educators are vigorously and easily engaged with each other through email, messages, video chat, online forums, social media, learning materials etc. Shortly, the educational arrangement environments are anticipated as mitigation to unexpected natural and mock pandemics such as Covid-19 in 2020 by the major changes connected with the digitalization of some portion of the system. It also allows educational programmes to be available 24/7 in dissimilar languages to carter to the varying requirements of the learners. Though digital education has supplementary benefits but it also has many prospect challenges in India. Worldwide, the digital revolution favored open access to information. Classrooms today have a lot of ICT resources almost all the teachers have made huge strides to incorporate digital technology to boost access to information and two-way activities for the learners. This article aims to give valuable perspectives of Information and Communication Technology and digital education into its future reimbursement, risks, and challenges of acceptance the latest technologies in the digital era, and vast online open courses. Further research and novelty in technology will restore the digital education system. Thus digital education will efficiently supports the classroom Challenges.

Issues in Curriculum Development in B. Ed

G. Lavanya
Student Teacher, 3rd Semester, Master of Education, RV Teachers College, Bengaluru, Karnataka,
Email: chinnari.guru@gmail.com

Abstract

Curriculum development for Bachelor of Education (B. Ed) programs plays a crucial role in shaping future educators and addressing the developing needs of the education sector. This paper examines key issues in curriculum development, including preparation with national educational standards, Lack of sequence in the curriculum, Overlapping of content, Outdated curriculum unavailability of books etc. Challenges such as insufficient participant engagement, limited resources, and the necessity for ongoing professional development for educators are also explored. By studying these factors, the study aims to highlight the importance of an active and responsive curriculum that not only prepares B.Ed. students for effective teaching but also promotes inclusive and equitable education. Recommendations for improving curriculum design and implementation are provided, emphasizing the need for cooperation among policymakers, educators, and institutions to foster a strong educational framework.

The Role of Emotional Resilience in Adapting to Emerging Educational Trends: A Study of B.Ed. Students in Mysuru District

Yogesha K A
Research Scholar, DOS in Education, KSOU, Mysuru, Email: ykasjce@gmail.com

Prof. N Lakshmi
Professor & Dean Academic, Karnataka State Open University, Mukthagangothri, Mysuru, Email:
shaibhat@yahoo.co.in

Abstract

This study investigates the role of emotional resilience in helping B.Ed. students navigate new educational trends in colleges within the Mysuru district. Utilizing a validated survey tool developed by Yogesh under the guidance of Prof. N Lakshmi, the research comprises 58 items and involves a sample of 78 B.Ed. students. The focus is on assessing how emotional resilience impacts adaptability to emerging educational practices, such as online learning, collaborative teaching, and inclusive education strategies. Findings indicate that higher levels of emotional resilience are positively correlated with improved adaptability, engagement, and academic performance among B.Ed. students. Students demonstrating strong emotional resilience reported better coping strategies when faced with challenges associated with new educational trends. Additionally, supportive peer relationships emerged as a significant factor in enhancing emotional resilience, contributing to a more positive learning environment. These insights highlight the necessity of integrating emotional resilience training into B.Ed. programs, ensuring that future educators are better equipped to adapt to evolving educational landscapes. By fostering emotional resilience, educational institutions can enhance the overall preparedness of teacher candidates, ultimately benefiting their future students and the broader educational community.

The Role of Reflective Practices in Teacher Education

Shilpa Shri R D
Research Scholar, Department of Studies and Research in Education, KSOU, Mysuru, Email:
smileeshri28@gmail.com

Abstract

In the context of future trends in education and teachers' Professional Development, The Reflective Practices (Thinking About the Way You Do Things) in Teaching if we consider the difficulties faced by the teacher during the teaching and learning process, how it will be resolved will be discussed in this paper. During the classroom transaction, the problems or challenges that the teacher faces can be identified, and several problems can be solved to cater to the needs of the students. In the professional development of teacher candidates, reflective practice is becoming an increasingly important operator and referent. The educational research has focused a great deal of emphasis on one aspect of pre-service teacher education: how teacher trainees think and learn from their practice. As a means of enhancing such abilities and knowledge and raising the caliber of one's work, Moore claims that reflective practice is more about the "skills needed to reflect constructively upon ongoing experience" (Moore, 2000: 128). An essential part of every educational system is teacher education. It is founded on a country's philosophy, culture, and character and is intimately related to society. Through the preparation of knowledgeable, committed, and professionally competent educators who can satisfy the needs of the system, teacher education promotes the improvement of education in schools.

Dilemmas and Disparities in the Implementation of the Language Policy: Challenges in the New Education Policy

Nishanth K N
Research Scholar, Department of P.G. Studies and Research in English,
Kuvempu University, Shankaraghatta, Karnataka, Email: nishanthkn03@gmail.com

Abstract:

The New Education Policy (NEP) has introduced a multilingual approach to education, aiming to promote linguistic diversity and inclusivity. The motive of the New Education Policy is to guide the enhancement of education in the subcontinent, considering the tradition and culture, and adopt its different stages at school and college education levels to make it effective. However, the implementation of this language policy faces numerous dilemmas and disparities, posing significant challenges to its success. This study investigates the obstacles hindering the effective implementation of the language policy, including inadequate infrastructure, insufficient teacher training, and socio-cultural barriers. The research employs different approaches and perspectives to examine the diverse educational settings. The research also wants to circle around the current status of the English language at the school level. It also attempts to critically analyse the implementation of policies throughout the country and to highlight and address the impeding cultural disparities and multilingual dilemmas to implement the New Education Policy effectively.

Awareness about Artificial Intelligence (AI) Tools in Education among the B.Ed. Trainees

K.S Srinivasa,
Assistant Professor, R.V. Teachers College (IASE) and Research Centre in Education, Bengaluru,
Email: srinivasa.rvtc@rvei.edu.in

Sahana Chatterjee
Student Teacher, M.Ed. R.V. Teachers College (IASE) and Research Centre in Education, Bengaluru,
Email: sahana.c2013@gmail.com

Abstract

Artificial Intelligence (AI) is taking over the world in most professional fields whether it is in medicine, engineering, security, business, or even in day-to-day household activity, AI is becoming a threat to people's jobs in different fields. The world wants a change towards betterment. Gen Z (1997-2012) and Gen Alpha (2013-2025) learners find learning challenging. They have less attention span (under extremely stressful conditions it is only 8-9 seconds) but their interest lies in innovation and digital usage. To make education an interesting and lifelong process, teachers should prepare the youth to meet the diverse national and global challenges for the present and the future. This study emphasizes the awareness of AI tools in education among the B.Ed. trainees. A survey has been conducted on B.Ed. trainees to give us an insight into whether they are aware of the enormous features that are provided by AI tools. Whether B.Ed. Trainees are ready to imbibe AI in their day-to-day education for learning or teaching, what are the different AI tools the B.Ed. trainees are aware of? And so on. Thus, this study will give us an understanding of the readiness of future teachers to inculcate AI in their classrooms.

Digital Education: Opportunities and Challenges

Smt. Gayathri K. J.
Assistant Professor, Mandavya College of Education, Mandya, Karnataka, India, Email:
gayathrikj.mys@gmail.com

Abstract

National Education Policy 2020 documented the significance of digital education in given that quality education for all. Education is the procedure of facilitating learning, attainment of knowledge, skills, principles, attitude, habits etc. to give in socio-economic enlargement of nation. Digital education is a multifaceted multidimensional topic which uses digital technology and tools in teaching and learning procedure. Digital education provides a lot of opportunities to both teachers as well to their students. Students as well as educators are vigorously and easily engaged with each other through email, messages, video chat, online forums, social media, learning materials etc. Shortly, the educational arrangement environments are anticipated as mitigation to unexpected natural and mock pandemics such as Covid-19 in 2020 by the major changes connected with the digitalization of some portion of the system. It also allows educational programmes to be available 24/7 in dissimilar languages to carter to the varying requirements of the learners. Though digital education has supplementary benefits but it also has many prospect challenges in India. Worldwide, the digital revolution favored open access to information. Classrooms today have a lot of ICT resources almost all the teachers have made huge strides to incorporate digital technology to boost access to information and two-way activities for the learners. This article aims to give valuable perspectives of Information and Communication Technology and digital education into its future reimbursement, risks, and challenges of acceptance the latest technologies in the digital era, and vast online open courses. Further research and novelty in technology will restore the digital education system. Thus digital education will efficiently supports the classroom Challenges.

Inquiry-Based Learning as a Strategy of Teaching Science

Mahadevi M Handral
Research Scholar, Dept of Education, Karnataka State Akkamahadevi Women University, Vijayapura, Email: madhuhandral99@gmail.com

Prof. U K Kulkarni,
Professor, Dept of Education, Karnataka State Akkamahadevi Women University, Vijayapura
e-mail: ukkulkarni1970@gmail.com

Abstract

Now a day's different innovative pedagogical strategies are using in education to make teaching learning process more effective. Teaching science through inquiry strategy leads to unfoldment of child's mind instead of stuffing it with dead material. Curiosity is an innate urge of human beings. Inquiry-based learning is a type of active learning that encourages students to ask questions, conduct research, and explore new ideas. This approach to learning helps students develop critical thinking, problem-solving, and research skills. The present paper focused on the concept and meaning of Inquiry based learning, the role of teacher in teaching by inquiry-based learning, need and scope of inquiry based learning in classroom learning activities. The present paper also tries to explain that how inquiry-based learning strategy that needs to be adopted or implemented.

Educational Policies for India

Prashant H
Assistant Professor of Sociology, SKHP Govt. First Grade College Hulkoti, Gadag, Email: prashant44h@gmail.com

Abstract

Globally, governments give education policy a lot of attention. Global pressure is putting more and more emphasis on how educational policies are performing and how they affect both social and economic development. Nonetheless, there is frequently a dearth of knowledge regarding the creation of educational policies and their definitions. An important historical development for the creation of Indian education policy was the introduction of western education. Prior to the development of contemporary education, only a very tiny percentage of people had access to learning possibilities. The Indian government created the National Policy on Education to encourage and oversee education in the country. India's program encompasses education from elementary school to university level in both rural and urban areas. Prime Ministers Indira Gandhi, Rajiv Gandhi and Narendra Modi issued the first, second and third NPEs on behalf of the Indian government, respectively, in 1968, 1986, and 2020.

Mobile Learning –A Modern Technology in Education

Murugeshi K
Research Scholar, Department of Education RCU, Belagavi, & Assistant Professor, B.E.A. College of Education, Davanagere, Karnataka, Email: murugeshik6@gmail.com.

Abstract

E-Learning and Mobile Learning (M Learning) serve distinct purposes in the realm of education and training. While e-Learning encompasses a broad spectrum of online learning conducted on various devices, M-Learning specifically tailors content delivery to mobile devices, emphasizing accessibility and flexibility. Mobile learning (m-learning) has become a quite significant factor in higher education. Central to mobile learning is its emphasis on the learner's mobility, providing them the freedom to decide when and where they engage with educational materials. As these devices are highly personalized and collaborative communication tools, they provide the institutions of tertiary education with flexible tools for complementing the existing technologies and extending the learning beyond the classrooms and homes from remote places like train or bus stations where students do not have any access to computers. This study focuses on best practices that show the value of these technologies by looking at different evaluation measures, like academic performance and accessibility. Mobile Apps for Teaching & Learning provides flexibility of usage, remote learning, high completion rates and utilization of free time, enjoyable and informal learning, and changing educational Standards

Innovative Teaching Practices and Methodologies in Teacher Education

Dr. Mahadevi B Tallur
Principal, KRCES's A B Patil College of Education,
Bailhongal District, Belagavi, Email: maharaj710@gmail.com

Abstract

The quality of educational process largely depends upon the quality of teachers. Though teaching is being considered as a science and a skill, basically it is a sublime art. Teacher education system is an important vehicle to improve the quality of school education. The revitalization and strengthening of the teacher education system is a powerful means for the upliftment of educational standards in the country. There are many issues that need urgent attention for improving the quality of teacher education programme. One of them is the need of innovations in teacher education programme. NPE (1986) stated "The existing system of teacher education needs to be overhauled or revamped." There are some resisting factors in our education system which prevents the teacher education institution from being innovative such as lack of physical facilities and funds, lack of diffusion of innovations among teacher educators, rigid framework, lack of research orientation etc. The biggest challenge any teacher faces is capturing the students" attention, and putting across ideas in such a way that it stays with them long after they have left the classroom .For this to happen, classroom experience should be redefined and innovative ideas that make teaching methods more effective should be implemented .So here are innovative ideas that will help teachers reinvent their teaching methods and make their classes interesting. Instead of taking the traditional lectures and textbooks route, modern teaching methods employ various innovative methodologies to keep students engaged and learning actively. Innovativeness means the ability to think beyond the boundaries and create something which is different from that which already exists. Without innovations, no progress is possible. Teachers have to be innovative and their grooming has to start from their training institutions.

In the present system of teacher education programme in India some of the innovative ideas to be practiced and focused they are: co-operative and collaborative learning, team teaching, reflective teaching, constructivism, blended learning, soft skills, Teacher-Centered Instruction. Small Group Instruction, Project-Based Learning. Inquiry-Based Learning. Flipped Classroom. education.

Challenges and Opportunities in Digital Education: Navigating the Future of Learning

Kumar D K

Research Scholar, P G Department of Studies in Education, Karnatak University, Dharwad, Email: kumarsavitha95@gmail.com

Abstract

Digital education has transformed the way knowledge is disseminated, with technology facilitating access to learning materials, fostering collaboration, and enabling personalized learning experiences. However, while digital education offers numerous opportunities for students and educators, it also presents significant challenges related to accessibility, equity, infrastructure, and pedagogical adaptation. This article explores the major challenges faced in digital education, the opportunities it presents for enhancing educational practices, and the future directions for digital learning in both developed and developing contexts. It provides a comprehensive analysis of the challenges and opportunities in digital education, focusing on the implications for learners, educators, and institutions. The exploration of future trends and recommendations for optimizing digital education is also discussed to help shape effective learning environments in the digital age. Understanding these dynamics is crucial for educators, policymakers, and stakeholders aiming to optimize the potential of digital education in diverse learning environments.

Technology-Assisted Student Assessment: Innovations, Implications, and Future Prospects

Magadum Hanamant Annappa
Research Scholar, PG Department of Studies in Education, Karnatak University, Dharwad, Email: hmagadum2@gmail.com

Abstract

Technology-assisted student assessment (TASA) refers to the use of digital tools and platforms to enhance and streamline the evaluation process, offering efficiency, real-time feedback, and personalized learning experiences. Technology-assisted student assessment is revolutionizing the educational landscape, offering new approaches to evaluating student learning and performance. The integration of technology into educational assessment has transformed traditional methods of evaluating student learning. This article explores how technology has transformed traditional assessment methods through innovations like automated testing, personalized feedback, learning analytics, and adaptive assessment systems. Additionally, it examines the potential challenges, such as equity, data privacy, and the role of educators in this tech-driven environment. It provides a comprehensive examination of the key technologies, benefits, challenges, and future directions in technology-assisted student assessments, highlighting its potential to enhance learning outcomes while addressing potential concerns regarding equity, data privacy, and the human element in education. The article concludes with a discussion of future prospects, outlining how technology might further shape the evolution of student assessment in educational settings.

Inclusive Education: Principles, Practices, and Challenges

Hanamant Fakeer Nayik
Research Scholar, PG Department of Studies in Education, Karnatak University, Dharwad,
Email: prajwal.hanuman@gmail.com

Abstract

Inclusive education is a transformative approach that seeks to provide equitable access to education for all learners, regardless of their abilities, socio-economic background, gender, race, or other individual characteristics. It aims to dismantle barriers to learning and participation while fostering diversity and inclusion in educational settings. By prioritizing diversity and equity, inclusive education challenges the traditional models of segregation and special education, promoting the idea that all children have a right to learn together. Despite growing global support for inclusive education, its implementation faces challenges, including limited resources, inadequate teacher training, and resistance to change. This article explores the principles and practices of inclusive education, discusses its benefits, and examines the barriers and potential solutions to ensure its successful integration into mainstream education systems worldwide. Moreover, it examines the barriers that hinder full inclusion, including systemic inequities, lack of resources, and insufficient teacher training, and offers recommendations for overcoming these challenges.

Value-Based Education Plays a Crucial Role in Fostering Wellbeing among Adolescents

Thrimurthy
Research scholar, DOS in Education, Davangere University, Davanagere,
Email: thrimurthyphdinedu@gmail.com

Dr. Venkatesha K
Professor, DOS in Education, Davangere University, Davanagere, Email:

Abstract

Globalization led to the emergence of high life style but deteriorated the Moral and Ethical values in society. Presently, we are witness to many social evils. Factors such as, blind race and cut-throat competition to accumulate money and things of leisure, has led to craving for Power and Pleasure. With the exposure to mass-media, our youth are blindly adopting other cultures, be it fashion, media or technology. Family disorganisation and quality of education has also led to deterioration of values. Our education system emphasises on materialistic achievements, thereby neglecting overall development of children. Value education program makes a significant impact on Personal, Social and Cultural Values in children. A good socio-emotional climate in school is vital. Teachers play an important role in imparting high ideals which can contribute in development of future society. It is not just the School or Teachers, the Society and Parents must also involve in this inculcation process to achieve overall wellbeing among adolescents. In this study, we try to explore the wellbeing process among adolescents through value education in detail.

Effectiveness of Life Skills Education on Problem-Solving Skill among Student - Teachers of B.Ed. programme

Dr. Asha G H
Principal, KSS College of Education, Davanagere, Karnataka,
Email: ashagh1185@gmail.com

Abstract

The present study is to find out the effectiveness of life skills education on Problem solving skill among student-teachers of B.Ed. programme. The study adopts "pre-test and post-test equivalent group experimental design." The sample of the study was 80 student-teachers of B.Ed. programme. The sample was randomly selected for the study and divides the sample as control and experimental group by conducting Emotional Intelligence Test. Each group consists of 40 student-teachers. The result reveals that, the pre-test Problem solving skill scores of student-teachers are similar in control and experimental group. The post-test Problem-solving skill scores of student-teachers are significantly higher in experimental group as compared to control group.

Innovative Teaching Practices and Methodologies in Education: Harnessing the Power of Experiential Learning

Sushma Janagouda
Research Scholar, Department of Education, Karnataka State Akkamahadevi Women's University, Vijayapur, Email: Sushma.janagouda22@gmail.com

Dr. Ganiger Bharati
Assistant Professor, Department of Education, Karnataka State Akkamahadevi
Women's University, Vijayapur.

Abstract

"Innovative Methodologies in Education: Harnessing the Power of Experiential Learning" explores how experiential learning methods enhance traditional education. Experiential learning involves active participation, where students engage with real-world scenarios, simulations, and hands-on activities. By doing so, students move beyond passive learning and develop critical thinking, problem-solving, and decision-making skills.

Innovative Methodologies in Education: Harnessing the Power of Experiential Learning" explores the dynamic shift from traditional teaching models to more immersive, student centered approaches. Experiential learning, rooted in the principle of learning through experience, fosters deeper understanding by engaging students in real-world problem-solving, collaboration, and reflective practice. This methodology enables learners to actively participate in their education, connecting theoretical concepts with practical application, which enhances retention and critical thinking skills. The paper examines various innovative strategies such as project-based learning, simulations, internships, and fieldwork, which empower students to develop autonomy and apply knowledge in meaningful contexts. These methods encourage creativity, adaptability, and emotional intelligence, aligning with the demands of a rapidly evolving workforce. Furthermore, experiential learning promotes interdisciplinary learning, where students explore connections across subjects, fostering a holistic educational experience. By integrating technology and personalized learning environments, educators can create flexible, interactive platforms that cater to diverse learning styles. The study highlights the importance of reflective assessment, where students analyse their experiences to gain insights into their learning process. Ultimately, the paper underscores the transformative potential of experiential learning in cultivating lifelong learners equipped with the skills necessary for success in both personal and professional domains.

Use of Yoga for Enhancing Academic Achievement

Mrs. Hemalatha,
Research Scholar, Department of Social Work, Karnataka State Akkamahadevi
Women University, Vijayapur Karnataka State India,
Email: hemalathanayak747@gmail.com

Dr. Gangadhar B. Sonar,
Department of Social Work, Special Officer, DPAR and Coordinator, Music Department Karnataka
State Akkamahadevi Women University, Vijayapura, Karnataka, India,
Email id: gbsonar@kswu.ac.in

Abstract

Yoga, a traditional practice from India, has evolved into a discipline that integrates physical, mental, and spiritual health. The current education system prioritizes high grades to meet job market demands, frequently neglecting moral and ethical education. This focus leads to significant challenges for students, including stress, anxiety; sleep disturbances, and an increased risk of suicidal thoughts. These changes put adverse impacts on student's academic performance. The inculcation of yoga is increasingly recognized as a valuable intervention for enhancing student health and well-being.

Objectives: This study aims to investigate the effects of academic pressure on student performance through secondary data and assess how yoga contributes to enhancing academic achievement. Additionally, it evaluates the impact of yoga programs implemented in schools on students' academic progress.

Methods: A detailed review of existing literature was carried out to understand the link between academic pressure and student health, the positive role of yoga, and the outcomes of yoga initiatives in school settings.

Results: The results highlight the yoga's positive impact on students, improving physical fitness, flexibility, and mental clarity. It enhances concentration, emotional stability, and cognitive function, helping manage academic stress. Overall, the results underscore yoga as an effective strategy for enhancing academic achievement, addressing the challenges presented by high academic demands.

Predicting the Future of Education

Usha Basavvagol
Assistant Professor, SGI, Shaikh College of Education, Belagavi,
Email: usha.basavvagol@rediffmail.com

Abstract

The education system has undergone significant development. One of the earliest formal education systems in India is the Gurukul system. Despite the ideas and knowledge that may have evolved, the fundamental structure has not changed. Earlier the students used to go to the Gurukuls. In a similar vein, students of today attend schools in order to take classes in a variety of disciplines. The focus of traditional education is on culture and customs and traditional teaching techniques place more emphasis on memorizing abilities. Whereas future trends in education focus on helping students develop and hone their skills. With rapid advancements in technology and shifts in societal needs, many are asking, "How do you think the education system will change in the future?" as we anticipate a move towards more personalized, flexible and technology driven learning environments. By staying informed about these future trends in education, educators and policymakers can better anticipate changes and adapt their strategies to ensure that they meet the evolving needs of students and prepare them for success in an increasingly dynamic world.

Innovative Teaching Practices and Methodologies

Akshata Kelaginamani
Assistant Teacher, KHPS Banki-Basarikatti Khanapur Belagavi, Email: akshatake189@gmail.com

Abstract

The landscape of education is rapidly evolving, driven by technological advancements, changing student needs, and shifts in pedagogical approaches. Innovative teaching methods are approaches to teaching and learning that prioritize students and emphasize interaction and engagement in the classroom. They can help students learn more effectively. Traditional teaching methods are outdated and need to be replaced with more interactive and engaging methods. Teachers needs to be creative and innovative and they should no longer be sole source of knowledge. Instead, they should guide and mentor students, and focus on problem-based learning. Innovative teaching methods are tailored to meet the individual needs of students, and help them learn more effectively. This paper explores the future of education by examining emerging trends and innovations in teaching and learning. It discusses the impact of digital technologies, personalized learning, Virtual reality technology, Using AI in education, 3D printing, Project based learning, Personalised learning, Gamification and so on. Their characteristics and tips to implement innovative teaching strategies. By embracing these trends and innovations, educators, teachers can create dynamic, engaging, and transformative learning experiences that prepare students for success in an increasingly complex and interconnected world.

Tools and Techniques for Digital Assessment in School Education

Smt. Deepu R
Assistant Teacher in English, Morarji Desai Residential School, Attibele, Anekal Taluk, Bengaluru, E-mail: deepukreis@gmail.com

Abstract

The emergence of digital assessment has not just modernized but revolutionized traditional methods of evaluating student performance, making it an integral part of contemporary school education. As technology continues to permeate education systems worldwide, digital assessment technologies empower instructors with unprecedented flexibility, efficiency, and customization in gauging learning outcomes. This abstract delves into the primary instruments and methods for digital assessment in educational settings, with a focus on their benefits, drawbacks, and potential for enhancement.

Digital technologies have changed several aspects of education, most notably how student learning is assessed. Digital assessment instruments offer student performance evaluation methods that are not only interactive and adaptable but also highly scalable. This scalability allows educators to efficiently assess large groups of students. This overview describes the main instruments and methods used in education to improve the efficiency, accuracy, and personalization of digital assessments in the classroom.

Challenges and Opportunities in Digital Education: A Path Forward

Dr. Basavaraj S,
Assistant Professor, Vivekananda B.Ed college, Arasikere Hassan, India.
E-mail: basavarajsiddu@gmail.com

Dr. Siddaraju,
Principal, Rajiv Gandhi College of Education, Bhadravathi, Shivamogga, India.

Abstract

Digital education has revolutionized learning, offering new paradigms for both educators and students. This article examines the dual facets of digital education, highlighting its significant challenges and abundant opportunities. Key challenges include issues of access and equity, content quality, student engagement, assessment methods, and the need for teacher training and support. Conversely, the opportunities presented by digital education encompass increased flexibility and accessibility, personalized learning experiences, global learning communities, innovative teaching tools, and data-driven insights. By addressing these challenges and harnessing the opportunities, stakeholders can foster an equitable and effective digital learning environment. Ultimately, collaboration among educators, policymakers, and communities is crucial in navigating this evolving landscape and shaping the future of education.

Teacher Education Institutions and National Education Policy 2020

Dr. S. S. Sammasagi,
Professor, Karnatak University College of Education, Dharwad.

Dr. Raghavendra V. Madalli
Assistant Professor, Shri Kumareshwar College of Education, Hangal, Haveri,
Email: kumbhikohalli@gmail.com

Abstract

The National Education Policy (NEP) 2020 represents a transformative approach to the Indian education system, with significant implications for Teacher Education Institutions (TEIs). This article examines the role of TEIs in the context of NEP 2020, highlighting the policy's emphasis on enhancing the quality of teacher education through reforms such as the introduction of Integrated Teacher Education Programs (ITEPs), the phasing out of substandard institutions, and the promotion of diverse learning modalities. NEP 2020 mandates a shift towards multidisciplinary and holistic education, integration of digital tools, and continuous professional development to produce highly competent and adaptive educators. The article explores the challenges and opportunities presented by these reforms and discusses the potential impact on the future of teacher education in India. By aligning TEIs with the NEP's vision, the policy aims to elevate the standard of education across the country and prepare teachers who are well-equipped to meet the demands of the 21st-century classroom.

Developing Emotional Intelligence

Geetha R G
Student Teacher, Master of Education, 3rd semester, RV Teachers College, Bengaluru, Karnataka,
Email: geetharg72@gmail.com

Abstract

Emotional Intelligence is the ability to recognize, identify, understand one's emotions and understand others feelings, behaviour patterns and realise how emotions affect people around us. Emotional Intelligence helps to manage healthier relationships among people. It fosters self-regulation in managing emotions and impulses, leading to better decision-making, team work, enhancing strong social skills, promoting better communication and goal orientation. Emotional Intelligence builds better personality, self-awareness, self-control and helps in developing internal motivation.

An emotionally intelligent approach to conflict resolution begins with self-awareness. This self-control creates a foundation for addressing conflicts constructively rather than reactively. An emotionally intelligent leader understands that one size does not fit all when it comes to managing people. They can adapt their communication and leadership style to suit different individuals and situations. By developing emotional intelligence, an individual can improve their resilience to overcome difficulties, suffering, can manage stress and achieve greater success in both personal life and professional career.

This presentation highlights the critical role of emotional intelligence in personal and professional development. It demonstrates how EI enhances self-awareness, relationship management, and leadership effectiveness.

Innovative Teaching Strategy: Synectic Model of Teaching, A Perspective

Dr. Janaki M
Assistant Professor, Dept of Education, KSOU, Mysuru, Email:

Smitha Rajendra
Research Scholar, Dept of Education, KSOU, Mysuru, Email: smitharajendra.09@gmail.com

Abstract

Education, in today's rapidly changing world has put forth many demands and challenges in front of educators. As a solution to this innovative teaching strategies have emerged. Introducing new teaching strategies proactively into the classroom is innovative teaching. Innovation in teaching helps students to attain their full potential. One such innovative teaching strategy is synectic model of teaching, which uses metaphor and analogy based techniques to encourage the use of divergent and convergent thinking to connect unfamiliar and familiar concepts. It is basically a creative thinking strategy that helps the students to understand the concepts in depth and foster higher order thinking, thus ensuring student-centered learning. This paper focuses on the theoretical foundation of synectic model of teaching, its strategies and application in educational context. This model of teaching not only stimulates imaginative thinking, it also enhances problem solving ability in students. Ultimately one of the main aim of education is to develop critical thinking and problem solving ability in the students which this model of teaching accomplish.

Gamification in Education: Implications and Challenges in Introducing Gamification in High Schools in Tamil Nadu

J. Ramesh Amalanathan
Ph.D. Scholar, Alagappa University College of Education, Alagappa University, Karikudi, Tamil Nadu, Email: ramieo2@aol.in

Dr. R. Portia
Assistant Professor, Alagappa University College of Education, Alagappa University, Karikudi, Tamil Nadu, Email: portiar@alagappauniversity.ac.in

Abstract

Gamification has become a widely used strategy in education to enhance student engagement, motivation, and academic success. This study examines both the benefits and challenges of applying gamification in Tamil Nadu's high school education. By incorporating game-based features like points, leaderboards, and rewards into the learning process, gamification aims to create a more dynamic and interactive classroom environment. However, several obstacles, such as limited technological resources, insufficient teacher preparedness, curriculum misalignment, and cultural views on gaming, complicate its integration in Tamil Nadu's schools. Using both qualitative and quantitative methods, the research identifies key factors that influence the effective implementation of gamification in the region. While the results highlight advantages such as increased student participation and personalized learning, they also reveal major challenges, including resistance from teachers, inadequate training, and a technology gap between urban and rural areas. The study provides practical recommendations for policymakers, educators, and other stakeholders to address these barriers, promoting a more innovative, student-focused approach to education in Tamil Nadu.

Creativity and Intelligence among Secondary School Students – A Study

Smt. Shilpa K S
Research Scholar, CMR University, Bengaluru, Karnataka, Email: ksshilpan@gmail.com

Dr. Balaji B R
Research Guide, & Professor of Education, School of Liberal Studies, CMR University, Bengaluru, Karnataka.

Abstract

Emotion of well-being and pleasure can be knowledgeable through creativity. One can take happiness in being creative for the sake of examination and discovery which has over generations improved human society's capability to stay alive in this impulsive globe, or one can put into practice creativity in the search of day to day activities or at work. Hence creativity is a major construct for promoting happiness. Is creativity associated to intelligence? The connection between creativity and intelligence has been subject to experimental research for decades yet there is no conformity on how these constructs are related. Therefore the main aspire of this research was to study to identify the level of creativity; to study the significant association between creativity and intelligence and to study the significant difference between secondary school boys and girls in Mysore south zone. In the present study survey method was adopted and purposive sampling techniques was employed, the total sample for the study was 60 out of which 30 boys and 30 girls. Present study recognized the ways and means of enhancing creativity and intelligence among secondary school students; revealed that there is a significant difference between secondary school boys and girls in their creativity; there is no significant difference between boys and girls in their intelligence and positively correlates between creativity and intelligence.

Current Practices of Swayam MOOCs in India

Dr. Ganiger Bharati
Assistant Professor, Department of Education and Research, Karnataka State Akkamahadevi Women's University, Vijayapura, Email: dreamz.bharti@gmail.com

Abstract

In the present era, the education system moving towards online courses. SWAYAM (Study of Web of Active learning for young Aspiring Minds) is an Indian online learning portal for MOOC

(Massive Open Online Course) platform. SWAYAM initiative was launched by Ministry of Human Resource Development (MHRD) and is providing innovative courses through its online portal. This paper discusses the current practices of SWAYAM MOOCs in India. SWAYAM National Coordinators and their role have been discussed and the overall student's enrollment, courses completed and exam registration. The researcher also discusses the different types of MOOCs in India. The study identifies certain challenges and benefits of using SWAYAM MOOCs in Indian platform.

A Study on Creativity and Ability for Comprehension of 9th Standard Students of Mysore Taluk

Dr. Chidananda A.L.,
Assistant Professor, Department of Studies and Research in Education,
Karnataka State Open University, Mukthagangothri, Mysore, Karnataka.
Email: friendlychidu@gmail.com

Abstract

The present study titled "A study on the Ability for Comprehension and Creativity of Ninth Standard Students of Mysore Taluk" is a descriptive survey study.

Education has proved to be useful in the development of human race. Number of components of education contribute for the growth and development of an individual. Among these some are the abilities developed within the individual and some other are the product of environment. Language plays an important role in the early childhood education in any educational system. Language is not only taught as a subject but is also used as the medium of instruction for teaching different school subjects right from the beginning. Language is the foundation of all our social relations for it is the primary medium by which we communicate our ideas and meaning to others.

Ability for Comprehension is the basic ability for an individual to have competency over different skills of language. Only when the child was the ability to comprehend what is heard, what is read, he or she will be able to continue in the process of communication. Unless this happen the individual fails to proceed in any social situation.

The Ability for Comprehension is basic for all day to day human endeavour, whether it is a medical clinic or a vegetable market or a stage of politician or a classroom. Ability for Comprehension is the minimum required trait of a person. The more the Ability for Comprehension better will be his involvement in social situations. Therefore, an attempt to develop the Ability for Comprehension among students at a very early age is an important task to be carried by an educationist. This task requires to analyse the factors that contribute for the Ability for Comprehension. Number of researches have been made on the development of the Ability for Comprehension at different stages of education. Primary, Higher Primary, Secondary and Higher Education.

Flipped Classroom Models

Shilpa Shri R D
Research Scholar, Dept of Studies and Research in Education, KSOU, Mysuru,
Email: smileeshri28@gmail.com

Nataraju M S
Research Scholar, Dept of Studies & Research in Education, KSOU, Mysuru,
Email: msnataraju72@gmail.com

Abstract

Information literacy training could benefit from the flipped classroom approach, which involves using class time for hands-on application exercises while electronic lectures are delivered to students at home. This article outlines many of the flipped classroom teaching style features and provides examples from the literature on library instruction and contemporary developments in higher education. The model's pedagogical advantages are emphasized, along with any possible drawbacks. There are other names for the flipped classroom, such as the inverted classroom and, more simply, the flip. While there are varying origin legends, the majority give credit to Colorado High School chemistry professors Jonathan Bergmann and Aaron Sams for being the first to use recorded lectures in 2006. The notion of hybrid, or blended, learning and problem-based learning—which use new technology and active learning strategies to engage students—led to the development of the flip. The two main features of the flipped classroom are the following: the practical application tasks, which were formerly homework, are brought into the classroom and the lecture is moved outside of the classroom, often via electronic means (Educause, 2012). There are several more alternative elements that, in my opinion, maximize this framework and provide pupils with better learning.

The What, How and Why of Solving Value Crisis

Dr N N Prahallada
Former Professor of Education, Regional Institute of Education, NCERT, Mysuru,
Email: nnprahallad@yahoo.co.in

Abstract

"It is quite common these days to find leaders in all sectors of society decrying the present climate of value crisis. Political, religious, social leaders and even educationalists point out that the country is going downhill because the people seem to have lost their moral integrity, sense of values, and that expediency has taken the place of pride as opposed to adherence of principles of conduct. They particularly point out that school students are growing up in a moral and spiritual vacuum.

The most urgent and significant reform needed is to transform not only the value system but also the basic structure and processes of the educational system. It will also imply the shifting of the emphasis from individual to social objectives, and from mere acquisition of information to the development of skills and character formation based on knowledge.

The problem of value education of the young has assumed increasing prominence in educational discussions during recent times. Parents, teachers and society at large are concerned about values and value education of children."

A Study of Machine Learning's Influence on Student Engagement and Achievement in AI-Driven Virtual Classroom

Dr. Radhika Kulkarni,

Teaching Assistant, Department of Education, Karnatak University, Dharwad, Karnataka, India, Email: mohangeeta05@gmail.com

Abstract

The main purpose of this study is to investigate the influence of machine learning on student engagement and achievement in AI-driven virtual classrooms, exploring differences based on gender, geographical location, and type of schools . A stratified random sample of 200 students from PU Colleges involved from Dharwad district. Standardized instruments measured student engagement and achievement. Statistical analysis revealed significant differences: girls and urban students demonstrated higher engagement and achievement rates, while private school students well performed than government school students. Machine learning tools predicted student engagement and achievement. Findings of the present study shows that there is a significant differences in students engagement levels and achievement between boys and girls, rural and urban, government and private school students in AI-driven virtual classrooms. Based on the findings the implications for educators and policymakers shown as, AI-driven virtual classrooms can enhance engagement and achievement for underrepresented groups. Targeted interventions should address existing gaps. Future research should investigate specific AI-driven features. The study highlights the importance of integrating machine learning-based adaptive assessments and personalized learning. Policymakers should promote equity and inclusivity. Schools can invest in machine learning tools. The study's findings inform strategies to promote equity and inclusivity in AI-driven virtual classrooms, ultimately enhancing the educational experience for diverse student populations. By exploring the intersection of AI, machine learning, and virtual learning environments, this research advances our understanding of the complex relationships between technology, teaching, and learning. The details of the study will be presented in the full length of the paper.

Need of English Language Education and Literacy among Students

Smt. Dakshayani Ashok Mandi

Research Scholar, Department of Studies in Education, Karnataka State Akkamahadevi Women's University Vijayapura, Email: dakshayanimandi@gmail.com

Dr. G. Sowbhagya

Assistant Professor, Department of Education, Karnataka State Akkamahadevi Women's University, Vijayapura

Abstract

English Language Education and Literacy refers to the process of teaching and learning English language skills, including reading, writing, speaking, listening, vocabulary development, grammar, and pronunciation. It aims to develop language proficiency, literacy skills, and cultural awareness, enabling individuals to communicate effectively, access information, participate in global communication, enhance career opportunities, and foster personal growth. English Language Education encompasses various teaching methodologies, including Communicative Language Teaching, Content and Language Integrated Learning, and Task-Based Language Learning. Literacy skills involve understanding various text types, critical thinking, and analytical skills. English Language Education is taught in primary, secondary, and higher education institutions, language schools, online platforms, and community centers, with assessment and evaluation methods including standardized tests, authentic assessments, self-assessment, and continuous feedback.

The Pros and Cons of Early Literacy Programme

Dr N N Prahallada

Former Professor of Education, Regional Institute of Education, NCERT, Mysuru, Email: nnprahallad@yahoo.co.in

Abstract

"The country as a whole looks upon Education as an omnipotent Instrument to bring meaningful changes in all sectors of life. This article focus mainly on Education of children from zero to six years which was neglected all these years. This is known as Early Literacy programme. The author of the Article worked in this Early Literacy Project of MHRD Flagship programme at RIE NCERT Mysore for three years as a Consultant. The NEP 2020 has also given lot of importance in its new school education formula of 5+3+3+4. This Article gives all importance to the mechanism of Early Literacy and its objectives. Whoever peruses this article will have a total understanding of Early literacy".

Impact of Self-Determination on Teacher Empowerment of Government-Upgraded School Relation to their Educational Qualification

Dr. Yashavantha. B,
Assistant professor, Mythri College of Education , Kuvempu University, Shivamogga, Karnataka, India.
E-mail: yashavanthsree@gmail.com

Abstract

Empowered teachers are more likely to innovate in their teaching methods, influence school policy, and effectively contribute to student success. One crucial factor influencing teacher empowerment is self-determination, which refers to an individual's ability to control their own actions and decisions. The present study attempts to study Impact of Self-Determination on Teacher Empowerment of Government Upgraded School Relation to Their Educational Qualification The objectives of the study To measure and analyse the levels of Self-Determination and Teacher Empowerment among government Upgraded School teachers with respect to Educational qualification, To study the relationship between Teacher Empowerment with Self-Determination among government Upgraded school teachers and study the mean significant difference in various components related to Self Determination among government Upgraded school teachers with respect to educational Qualification. The study was a descriptive survey in order to know Impact of variables. It is correlational and casual-comparative in nature and comprised 405 teachers out of the total pool of 756 teachers. This study clearly showed that the majority of the teachers fall under average level of self-determination. Teacher Empowerment and Self-Determination of Upgraded School Teachers have a Significant Relationship This study is inferred that "there is a Mean significant differences between in self-determination among government upgraded school teacher with respect to their Educational qualification" Impact of Educational Qualification on Self-Determination the significant difference in self-determination scores based on qualifications ('F'=10.246, p<0.05) highlights the importance of teachers' educational background in shaping their motivation and empowerment and Enhancing teacher self-determination can thus lead to better academic performance and a more positive educational experience for students.

The Psychology Behind Gamification: Increasing Intrinsic Motivation in Educational Settings

Dr. Kiran Kumar K S
Assistant Professor, Kumadvathi College of Education, Shikaripura, Email:
kirankumbar.ks25@gmail.com

Abstract

Gamification, the application of game-design elements in non-game contexts, has become an increasingly popular strategy in educational settings. It leverages the motivational aspects of games to engage learners, fostering both intrinsic and extrinsic motivation. This paper explores the psychological mechanisms behind gamification and its impact on increasing intrinsic motivation in educational environments.

At the heart of gamification is the theory of intrinsic motivation, which is driven by an individual's internal desire for mastery, autonomy, purpose, and relatedness. Points, badges, leaderboards, and other game mechanics are discussed as tools to satisfy the need for competence, by providing clear goals and immediate feedback, as well as the need for autonomy, by offering students choices and the ability to navigate their learning paths. Additionally, elements such as collaborative challenges address the need for relatedness by fostering social connections among learners.

While gamification can successfully boost motivation, there is a fine line between using game elements to encourage intrinsic motivation and fostering a reliance on extrinsic rewards, which may undermine long-term engagement. The paper discusses the potential risks associated with over-reliance on extrinsic motivators like rewards and competition, which can diminish the self-driven aspect of learning. This highlights the importance of designing gamification systems that prioritize intrinsic motivators, ensuring that game mechanics enhance, rather than replace, the inherent satisfaction of learning.

The paper concludes with recommendations for educators and designers on how to create gamified learning experiences that nurture a deep, lasting engagement with educational content by tapping into learners' intrinsic motivations, ultimately promoting better learning outcomes and a more enjoyable educational experience.

By blending psychological insights with practical strategies, this paper contributes to the ongoing discussion on optimizing gamification for educational purposes.

Encouraging a Healthy Work-Life Balance as Part of Career Development Programs

Dr. Kiran Kumar K S
Assistant Professor, Kumadvathi College of Education, Shikaripura,
Email: kirankumbar.ks25@gmail.com

Abstract

In today's fast-paced and increasingly interconnected world, the boundary between work and personal life is becoming increasingly blurred. As the demands of the modern workforce evolve, there is growing recognition of the importance of work-life balance for long-term productivity, personal well-being, and job satisfaction. This abstract explores the critical role that educational institutions and career development programs play in preparing students to navigate this challenge, ensuring they enter the workforce equipped not only with technical and professional skills but also with the tools to maintain a healthy balance between work and life.

The traditional view of career development often emphasizes skill acquisition, job readiness, and professional networking, but it rarely addresses the potential risks of burnout, stress, and work-life imbalance. This oversight can have serious long-term consequences for individuals and organizations alike, including mental health issues, decreased productivity, and high employee turnover. Therefore, integrating work-life balance principles into career development programs is not only essential for individual well-being but also for fostering a more sustainable and productive workforce.

This paper will explore several key strategies for promoting work-life balance within educational frameworks: a) Incorporating Time Management and Self-Care into Curricula, b) Fostering Flexibility and Remote Work Awareness, c) Modeling Work-Life Balance through Institutional Policies, d) Addressing the Role of Employers in Supporting Work-Life Balance

In conclusion, preparing students for the future workforce involves more than just technical competence; it requires fostering the skills and mindset needed to maintain a healthy work-life balance.

As the nature of work continues to evolve, career development programs must prioritize the integration of these principles to ensure students can achieve both personal fulfillment and professional success in their careers. By embedding work-life balance into the foundation of career education, institutions can contribute to the development of resilient, productive, and satisfied professionals who thrive in all aspects of their lives.

An Effective Development of Web Content Packages Using eXeLearning Authoring Tool for Student-Teacher

Dr. Tahseen Taj

HOD, KSS M.Ed. College. Davangere, Email: taj.tahseen828@gmail.com

Abstract

A web-based learning environment certainly encompasses a technological element, as the majority of learning activities are conducted through the medium of the computer. Availability of and easy access to a learning environment are initial requirements, as an effective web-based learning situation must support anytime, anywhere learning Moreover, interface design is critical, as it determines the usability of the learning environment. Interface design should focus on ease of learning, ease of use and aesthetic. The rapid development of ICT has provided a strong technical platform that makes constructivist learning via the Internet and MOOCS more feasible and easier to implement more opportunities in web-based learning context in one learning platform. This study explores about the theory of Vygotsky social constructivist learning perspectives can be used in the design, development, and implementation of Web-based learning environments (WBLEs) through open access software eXelearning Authoring tool. eXelearning is a software used to create educational interactive web contents. It gives a dynamic interactive web context based on the social constructivist theory and based on ADDIE model for the design and development of web content . The purpose of this study is to develop and study the Effect of web content packages for the Student Teacher.

Develop and Study the Effectiveness of Web-Based E-Learning Course on Learning and Teaching Process for Student Teacher of B.Ed. Programme

Dr. Tahseen Taj

HOD, KSS M.Ed. College. Davangere, Email: taj.tahseen828@gmail.com

Abstract

Web-based Learning is an advanced system and powerful tool which supports teaching and learning by the use of an Information and communication technology. It bridges the gap between a teacher and a student in different geographical location. Web-based Learning is the use of technology to enable people to learn anytime and anywhere. This study examines the effectiveness of web-based e-learning course specially designed web online course which focuses on the socio constructivist approaches as a medium of learning in the Teacher education. Web-based e-learning courses provide convenience for students in learning activities such as increasing productivity, flexible and interactive. An experimental study was conducted to know the effectiveness of web-based e-learning package on learning and teaching process. The ADDIE model was adopted to design and develop the web-based e-learning package. An eXelearning software was applied to prepare the web content and provided interactive activities. The complete web-based e-learning package was developed based on the social constructivist principles of learning. The experimental group was taught with web-based e-learning course and the control group were taught with conventional method. Pre-test and Post-test were administered independent sample t-test was used to analyze the data at the probability level of 0.01. The findings of the study showed that the web-based e-learning course was more effective than the conventional learning method in terms of developing knowledge construction, Collaborative interaction, Self-regulated learning and web self-efficacy. Thus, it is concluded that the web-based e-learning course is effective for learning than the conventional method in the teacher-education.

Teacher Leadership and Mentorship

Dr. Shivakumar Sthavarmath
Assistant Professor, K.C.T College of Education, Kalaburagi-585105, Karnataka,
Email: sskumar428@gmail.com

Abstract

This paper focuses on teachers' voices, their knowledge building, and teacher leadership—an essential aspect of the work of the Leadership for Learning Network, which is the subject of this special issue. How these ideals are put into practice enables educators to take the lead in innovation and advance the field of professional knowledge. While the caliber of instruction has a significant impact on student motivation and accomplishment, it has long been maintained that the caliber of leadership has an impact on teacher motivation and caliber of instruction in the classroom. Beyond the confines of their classrooms, teacher leaders take on the difficulties of enhancing their teaching methods by collaborating with their peers, school administration, professional staff, and students and their families. The fact that "leadership" is not a job title or position is one of the ambiguities in defining and recognizing teacher leaders. Being a "team leader" is not the same as being a teacher leader; in most schools, there are teachers who are the appointed leaders of their grade level teams or departments.

Challenges and Opportunities in Digital Education

Dr. Ruksana Anjum. M. A.
Assistant Professor, Sri. D. Devraj Urs First Grade College,
Honnur, Gollarahatti, Davangere.

Abstract

The significance of digital education in delivering high-quality education to all has been recognized by National Education Policy 2020. The process of supporting learning and the acquisition of information, skills, attitudes, beliefs, habits, etc. in order to support the socio-economic development of a country is known as education. Utilizing digital technologies and tools in the teaching and learning process, digital education is a multifaceted and complicated subject. There are a lot of opportunities in digital education for both teachers and students. Through social media, online forums, video chat, email, messaging, and other methods, educators and students are readily and actively connected with one another. Digital education offers enhanced accessibility, modification, and adaptability in terms of course content for students. It improves mobility, interactivity, engagement, and motivation in the learning process. Additionally, it permits educational programs that are available continuously in several languages to fulfill students' various demands.

While there are plenty of advantages to digital education, India will face multiple challenges in the future. The development of effective online content, its digital repository, and the method of delivery to learning students through the effective infrastructure and technology are the main problems in the new era of digital education. The digital education system will be updated with further technological innovation and research. As a result, digital education will continue to effectively assist classroom instruction both now and in the future.

Innovative Teaching Practices in Secondary Education

Dr. Ruksana Anjum. M. A.
Assistant Professor, Sri. D. Devraj Urs First Grade College,
Honnur, Gollarahatti, Davangere.

Abstract

The 21st century is a creative and disastrous time. India requires a vast amount of educated labor. The most effective ways to enhance the necessary abilities for teachers and students must be found because the conventional teaching and learning approach is out of date. To promote long-lasting and employability skills, there is an urgent need to shift methodology from fact-based traditional lecture to interactive education. Teaching and learning innovation are now crucial to solving this issue. Using the many approaches and strategies that are discussed in the paper will assist in achieving the intended result. This article outlines the unique approaches of instruction that the nation's secondary education institutions are implementing.

Study on the Teacher Leadership Qualities Perceived by Student Teachers of Four-Year Integrated Teacher Education Programme-BA.BEd & B.Sc.BEd

Dr.Lokesh T N,
Head & Co-ordinator, Dept of Education, NMKRV College for Women, Bengaluru, Email: lokeshtn.nmkrv@rvei.edu.in

Abstract

The quality of nation obviously depends on quality of education imparting. Thats why there is a great need of well defined and qualitative education which can reach each and everyone. To succeed in this mission there is a need of teachers who can capable of leading all the students like a leader. In order to do this teachers should have leadership qualities. Current situation emphasize the importance of teacher leaders who can impress and sincerely value the student and become a model and guide in the process of learning and production in order to be successful in the transformation and development of the educational organizations and nation at large.

The aim of this study is to explore the teacher leadership qualities as perceived by student teachers enrolled in the four-year integrated teacher education programs, B.A,B.Ed and B.Sc,BEd. The study sample includes 83 student teachers from these programs. A tool specifically designed by the researcher was used to gather data on teacher leadership qualities, which was then analysed using appropriate statistical methods.

Effectiveness of Psychological Wellbeing through Mindfulness Education: A Study among Secondary School Students in Bengaluru City

Dr. Vishwanatha K.
Assistant Professor, Acharya Institute of Graduate Studies, Bengaluru,
Email: drvishwanathak1326@gmail.com

Abstract

Mindfulness learning has appeared as a capable approach to promote psychological wellbeing among students as well as learning outcome. This research investigates the impact of mindfulness education on students' psychological wellbeing at secondary education level. To examine the effectiveness of mindfulness education in enhancing psychological wellbeing, reducing stress, and improving emotional regulation among secondary school students. A sample of 100 students age range between 14 to 16 will participate. Mindfullness Education studied as independent variable, Psychological Wellbeing studied dependent variable along with moderating variables (sex and type of management). The **Psychological Well-Being Scale (PWBS)** developed by Dr. Devendra Singh Sisodia and Ms. Pooja Choudhary (2012) and the Mindful Attention Awareness Scale (MAAS) developed by Kirk Warren Brown and Richard M. Ryan (2003) will find out the psychological wellbeing and mindfulness education levels. Statistical techniques like Mean, SD, correlation and independent 't' test will include for the proposed study. The result aims to show a positive significant relationship between psychological wellbeing and mindfulness education, showing the important role of mindfulness education in improving psychological wellbeing and academic performance.

Role of Social-Emotional Intelligence in Student Academic Success

Smt. Huchchannavar Sudha Sharanaraddi
Research Scholar, Department of Studies in Education, Karnataka State Akkamahadevi women University, Vijayapura, Email: sudharaddi84@gmail.com

Dr. G Sowbhagya
Assistant Professor, Department of Education, Karnataka State Akkamahadevi Women University, Vijayapura, Email:

Abstract

Social and Emotional Learning (SEL) is crucial for students' academic success, enabling them to develop essential skills such as self-awareness, self-management, social awareness, relationship skills, and responsible decision-making. By incorporating SEL into their education, students experience improved academic performance, better attendance and engagement, increased motivation, enhanced critical thinking and problem-solving, reduced stress and anxiety, and improved relationships with peers and teachers. Effective SEL teaching strategies include explicit instruction, integration with academic subjects, project-based learning, role-playing, mindfulness, and service-learning projects. Assessing SEL involves surveys, observations, performance tasks, and standardized assessments. Despite challenges such as teacher training and resource allocation, best practices like school-wide SEL initiatives, teacher-student relationships, family involvement, and continuous professional development can foster a supportive learning environment. Organizations like Collaborative for Academic, Social, and Emotional Learning (CASEL) and National Association of School Psychologists (NASP) provide valuable resources for implementing effective SEL programs, ultimately leading to improved academic outcomes and lifelong success.

Role of Emotional Intelligence in improving Academic Achievement: A Correlational Study of Secondary School Students

Nakshtra D.
Research Scholar, Department of Studies in Education, Karnatak University,
Dharwad, Email: nakshtrasmg@gmail.com

Dr. R.H. Naik
Assistant Professor, University College of Education, Karnatak University, Dharwad.

Abstract

This research paper aims to investigate the role of emotional intelligence (EI) in enhancing the academic achievement of students at secondary education level, focusing on the relationship between EI and academic achievement. The proposed research will adopts a descriptive survey method, with a sample of 100 9th standard students selected through stratified random sampling from six schools in the Bengaluru North Educational Division. The Emotional Intelligence Scale by Anukool Hyde and Sanjyot Pethe (2002) was employed to assess students' EI studied as independent variable, while academic achievement data were collected from school office records studied as dependent variable. Background variables include gender (boys and girls) and type of management (government, private aided/unaided). The obtained data will be analyzed by using statistical techniques namely mean, standard deviation, correlation and independent 't' test, with a significance level set at 0.05. The results reveal a positive significant correlation between emotional intelligence and academic achievement, suggesting that students with higher emotional intelligence tend to perform better academically. Moreover, the study highlights the importance of incorporating emotional intelligence instruction into the school curriculum to improve students' overall performance. This research contributes to the emergent evidence that emotional intelligence is a serious factor in academic success and calls for educational policies that highlight emotional learning as part of overall student development.

Promoting Research, Innovation and Excellence for
Future Education in India

Dr Aparna J Shinde,
Assistant Professor, Sidhartha Law College, Kalaburgi, Email: aparnamaley@gmail.com

Abstract

Education means transformation. Understanding the word is understands the world. The universities as the makers of the future cannot persist in the old patterns. The importance of higher education is for national welfare. The purpose of all education is to provide a coherent picture of the universe and an integrated way of life. Man cannot live by a mass of disconnected information. He has a passion for an ordered intellectual vision of the connections of things. The aim of education is at the development of the individual, the discovery, training and utilisation of his special talents.

In a science-based world, education and research are crucial to the entire developmental process of a country, its welfare, progress and security. It is characteristic of a world permeated by science that in some essential ways the future shape of things is unpredictable.

Many recent reports from UNESCO, the OECD, the World Bank, the World Economic Forum, and the Brookings Institution have highlighted that the. Students must develop cognitive skills & ' foundational skills' of literacy and numeracy and 'higher-order' cognitive skills such as critical thinking and problem solving skills - but also social and emotional skills, also referred to as 'soft skills', including cultural awareness and empathy, perseverance and grit, teamwork and leadership. India is a country having strong knowledge societies that attained their intellectual and material wealth in large part through science as well as art, language, and culture that enhanced and uplifted not only their own civilisations but those around the globe. If India is to become a leader in research areas, and truly achieve the potential of its vast talent pool to become a leading knowledge society in the coming years and decades, the nation will require a significant expansion of its research capabilities and output across disciplines. Research has more essential for the economic, intellectual, societal, environmental, and technological health and progress of a nation.

Effectiveness of Music Integrated Approach to Education: An Analysis of TED Talks

Bhagyalakshmi. A
Research Scholar, Department of Studies in Education, University of Mysore,
Manasagangothri, Mysuru, Email: bhagyathestudent@gmail.com

Prof. Dr. Sheela G
Chairperson, Department of Studies in Education, University of Mysore,
Manasagangothri, Mysuru, Email:

Abstract

Music Integration, an approach to Education can help students learn new concepts in a joyful and engaging way. Research reports highlighting the importance of Music Integration to Education are available in various forms. Technology, Entertainment and Design talks, popularly known as TED talks disseminate the knowledge and works of expert speakers across the globe on various topics like education, science, technology, creativity and business through influential videos.TED is a non-profit which discovers and spreads ideas that spark conversation and drive meaningful change through deepened understanding. TED talks do not use difficult jargons and rather the language of speakers is informal and humorous sometimes. They convey knowledge to a wider audience. Hence they qualify as a novel genre of educational resources.

The present paper is aimed to analyze the deductions and conclusions of some of the experts who spoke on the importance of Music in cognitive development of children and its advantage to include in school curriculum. 10 TED talks from YouTube which speak about the Music Integrated Approach to Education at school level are selected as purposive sample and are analysed qualitatively. The results show why and how Music Integrated Approach to Education is effective.

The Impact of STEAM Education on 21st Century Skill Development

Manjula Hadimani

Student Teacher, Master of Education, 3rd Semester, RV Teachers College, Bangalore, Email: mmkiragi@gmail.com

Abstract

STEAM education, incorporating Science, Technology, Engineering, Arts, and Mathematics, represents an innovative shift in modern teaching Example. Unlike traditional STEM approaches, which covers the area of technical skills, STEAM highlights creativity and critical thinking by integrating the Arts. This multilayered model assists a holistic educational experience that encourages students to think beyond standard academic boundaries.

By using inquiry-based and project-based learning, STEAM nurtures students' curiosity, innovation, and collaboration. Students engage in real-world problem-solving, where science and technology are applied alongside artistic expression, standard a deeper understanding of both technical and creative concepts. For instance, a STEAM project might involve designing a sustainable city, blending architectural creativity with environmental science and technological tools.

The main benefits of STEAM education are more extensive . It increases student's creative thinking , problem solving , collaboration with each other and critical thinking abilities. It also engages underrepresented groups, particularly in STEM fields, by offering a more inclusive, engaging approach to learning. However, challenges such as the need for teacher training, resource constraints, and the development of new assessment of the existing models.

Looking ahead, STEAM education will play a crucial role in preparing students for future careers that demand both technical expertise and creativity. As the global workforce increasingly values innovation, the integration of the Arts with STEM subjects ensures that students are not only proficient in technical skills but also capable of thinking critically and creatively to solve complex challenges.

New Trends and Challenges in Physical Education and Sports

Channabasappa N Soratur

Physical Education Director, Priyadarshini First Grade College, Rattihalli Haveri, Karnataka,
Email: cnsoratur06@gmail.com

Abstract

This paper aims to identify the current trends and challenges in physical education and sports and based on these current challenges, future trends and challenges would be discussed. There are various factors which are diminishing the interest of students in physical education activities. Although the physical education is being taught as a part of curriculum in all the schools but lack of adequate time and trained teachers, good facilities are responsible for little interest in this field. The future challenges to make this field interesting involves an adequate curriculum, sufficient funds allotment for holding various competitions and role of technology to create awareness about the importance of physical activities and sports in our daily life. All these issues have been discussed in the present study.

New Trends in Physical Education and Sports

Sathish Kumar K R

College Director of Physical Education, Government First Grade College, Sullia, South Canera District (Karnataka) Email: sathishped1@gmail.com

Abstract

Physical Education and Sports forms an important part of education even when it never received the importance it deserves. Even though it is included as part of the curriculum from the early stages of education, it has never been taken seriously by the educational administrators, the academicians and the students. Physical Education is the only profession where you talk as well as perform. The concept of Physical Education in the mind of the general public is big round, play and play and no work. Abraham Lincoln quoted in one of his address, "Sportsman is the best Ambassador of the Nation." Hence, the Physical Education Director, Teacher can also be the best Ambassador of Institution, University. At present compare to earlier years and now we can come across the decline of physical education in education compare to present is one needs to overcome the hurdles and battles to improve the structure and infrastructure status in around to develop the overall discipline in physical education and sports.

A Study on Self-Concept of Children with Special Needs in Relation to Academic Achievement at Secondary Level

Dr. Sushma R.
Assistant Professor, P.G Department of Education, Rani Channamma University, Belagavi,
Email: sushmarcueducation@gmail.com

Abstract

The present study attempted to investigate the predictive correlates of academic achievement of secondary school special needs students. To attain this academic achievement was considered as the criterion variable, independent variables such as self-concept and a few background variables such as Gender, type of school management, and locality were selected. The study was constituted with a Purposive sampling technique of special needs students drawn from various secondary schools of Dakshina Kannada district (Urban and Rural) recognized by the State Government of Karnataka representing three types of management (private, aided and government) giving representation to locality (rural and urban), Gender (male and female). For the present study the descriptive analysis 't' test, One-way ANOVA (F Test), and Two-way ANOVA, were applied to achieve the objectives. Data was collected by a self-constructed tool and analysed with the help of SPSS package. The findings of the study show that Positive high degree correlation exists between Academic Achievement and Self-Concept among Secondary School Children with special needs it can be concluded that the students with good self-concept do possess better Academic Achievement. Self-concept between government and aided schools". It is inferred that, there is no difference in Self-concept among types of school management Children with Special Needs. It is inferred that there is no difference in Self-Concept between rural and urban Secondary School Children with Special Needs. Self-concept between male and female schools". It is inferred that there is no difference in Self-Concept between male and female Secondary School Children with Special Needs.

Outstanding Features of NEP 2020 for Higher Education

Smt. Ashwini K
Research Scholar, Karnataka State Akkamahadevi Women's University, Vijayapura &
Assistant Professor, Kuvempu Shatamanotsava Shikshana Mahavidyalaya, Shivamogga
Email: arsannidhi16@gmail.com

Dr. G. Sowbhagya
Assistant Professor and Research Guide, Department of Education
Karnataka State Akkamahadevi Women's University, Vijayapura

Abstract

In an era where education is the cornerstone of progress, the National Education Policy (NEP) 2020 emerges as a game-changer for higher education in India. This comprehensive framework aims to revamp the educational landscape and align it with contemporary global standards. In this article, we will explore the outstanding features of NEP 2020 that promise to transform higher education into a more accessible, inclusive, and enriched experience for aspiring students. And the National Education Policy 2020 stands as a testament to India's commitment to advancing higher education. With a focus on flexibility, multilingualism, technology integration, research and inclusiveness, NEP 2020 not only aims to enhance the learning experience but also prepares students for the challenges of tomorrow.

A Study on Awareness about Digital Literacy among Secondary School Students

Dr. Lavanya C.E.
Assistant Professor, National College of Education,
Shivamogga, Email: celavanyahemanth@gmail.com

Abstract

The advent of the digital age has brought significant changes to education, requiring students to develop digital literacy skills. This study has examined the level of awareness of digital literacy among secondary school students, with a focus on gender and locality differences. The research was conducted on a sample of 200 students using stratified sampling techniques, encompassing both urban and rural schools. A structured questionnaire was used as the research tool to gather data on digital literacy awareness. Statistical analysis revealed a significant difference in digital literacy awareness based on gender and locality. The study highlights the urgent need for digital literacy initiatives in secondary education, especially for students from rural areas.

Teachers Professional Development

Rukmini. K
Assistant Professor, S.J.G B.Ed. College, Anandapura, Email:

Karunakara. N N
Principal, S.J.G B.Ed. College, Anandapura, Email:

Abstract

Teachers' Professional Development is Defined as activities that develop the skill, knowledge, experience and other characteristics of teacher. Teacher Professional learning is a complex process which requires cognitive and emotional involvement of teachers individually and collectively, teachers Professional Development (PD) is crucial to improving students outcomes because PD involves a multi-dimensional structure and changes across a teachers Professional life. Our educators needed to update their knowledge in emerging technologies such as all, and Skill for adapting to new modes of teaching teachers ongoing learning has a significant impact on their teaching. It is not always easy for them to be motivated and willing to change for the best. Effective professional Development provides teachers with adequate time to learn, practice, implement, and reflect upon new strategies that facilitate changes in their practice. I discussed the best ways for teachers to improve their performance in teaching and how that can effect their students learning. PD is important because it helps teachers keep up with changing educational needs and wider world it also helps teachers develop the skills and expertise they need to become better teachers. Professional Development is learning to earn or maintain Professionals such as academic degrees to formal course work, conferences and informal learning opportunities situated in practice.

A Study on Relationship Between Emotional Intelligence and Academic Achievement

Dr K.T. Nagaraj Naik,
Principal, M.M. College of Education Davangere, Email: mmceedn@gmail.com

Abstract

Emotional intelligence describes the ability, capacity, skill, or self-perceived ability to identify, assess, and manage the emotions of one's self, of others, and of groups. Emotional intelligence refers to the ability to perceive, control, and evaluate emotions. Emotional intelligence is described by the capability to understand emotions, recognize emotions, help thought to build from emotions and skill to control emotions which leads to intellectual development . Emotional intelligence helps individuals to grow intellectually and helps in achieving milestones at workplace. The primary purpose of the research is to measure the association between academic achievement & emotional intelligence of the post-graduate management students. The total number of 200 undergraduate. students of Davangere University has been selected for measuring relationship between academic achievements & emotional intelligence. The primary data has been collected by Emotional Intelligence Scale. Correlation model have been used for fulfilling the objective of the research. The major outcomes of the study are that the six dimensions of emotional intelligence shows positive relationship with academic achievement and only one of the dimensions have a negative correlation with the same. Positive expressivity dimension is the best predictor in explain the academic achievement while the other dimensions are also suggested as significant predictors.

Significance of Life Skills Education for Lifelong Learning

Annapurna A
Research scholar, Karnataka State Open University, Mukthagangothri, Mysuru.
Email: annapurnaa145@gmail.com

Dr. N. Lakshmi
Professor & Dean Academic, Karnataka State Open University, Mukthagangothri, Mysuru, Email: shaibhat@yahoo.co.in

Abstract

At present world is changing constantly. Everyone is struggling completely to adopt themselves to this changing environment. A set of skills required to adopt the changing scenario. Among those skills life skills are invaluable assets that can help everyone to navigate the challenges of daily living. So educational institutions from the beginning to the higher level need to provide life skills education to cope with challenges and prepare students to face the changing world. Life skills in higher education bridge the gap by integrating practical skills which are essential to navigate their personal and professional lives successfully. Life skills education helps attain various skills which makes an individual competent and capable to face the challenges in the life. In this article it is discussed in detail to find the importance of Life skills education in lifelong learning.

Innovative Teaching Methods in Secondary Education and its Benefits for Preparing Teachers for Future Trends in Education

Dr. Vijaya Shivaputrappa Agadi

Assistant Professor, Vivekananda College of Education, Arsikere,

Hassan District, Email: vijayagadivce@gmail.com

Abstract

Innovative teaching approaches in secondary education serve an important role in altering traditional pedagogy, preparing both teachers and students for future academic and professional challenges. This research investigates how several innovative techniques, such as technology integration, experiential learning, individualized education, and collaborative methods, can improve student engagement, critical thinking, and creativity. In India, notably in Karnataka, many schools are employing flipped classrooms, project-based learning (PBL), and inclusive education practices to encourage personalized learning environments. These strategies not only encourage academic success, but they also help students acquire important life skills like communication, problem-solving, and flexibility. Furthermore, professional development programs such as Continuous Professional Development (CPD) and Professional Learning Communities (PLCs) help teachers embrace and facilitate these new teaching techniques. While novel methods have numerous advantages, like greater student participation, retention, and emotional intelligence, they also present obstacles. Resistance to change, limited resources, and the need for continual teacher training are common roadblocks. Nonetheless, by embracing contemporary technologies such as artificial intelligence (AI), virtual reality (VR), and social-emotional learning (SEL), educators can foster a dynamic, inclusive, and future-ready educational environment. This article proposes for a transition from teacher-centered to student-centered learning in secondary school to ensure that students are not just taught knowledge but also prepared to manage an increasingly complicated and changing environment.

Internationalization of Higher Education in India: Status, Challenges and Opportunities

Dr. U K Kulkarni

Professor, Department of Education, Karnataka State Akkamahadevi Women University, Vijayapura,

Email: ukkulkarni1970@gmail.com

Abstract

This article discusses the need and changing wants associated with internationalization of higher education in Indian context. The demand for international education is growing day by day. To cater these needs, institutions have started to take new steps. Besides traditional providers of higher education, new knowledge providers from business houses have started developing innovative models for delivery of higher education. India has certain advantages to expand its internationalization initiative and as a result receiving interests from foreign universities for setting up campuses in the country. India needs to have a policy towards private higher education including foreign universities desirous of setting up campus in India.

Developing Emotional Intelligence through Inculcating Values in Education

Dr. Kanakappa Pujar
Assistant Professor, Department of Education, Rani Channamma University, Belagavi, Karnataka,
Email: dr.kanakappa.pujar@gmail.com

Rasana Hulamani
Research Scholar, Department of Education, Rani Channamma University, Belagavi, Karnataka,
Email: rasanahulamanis16@gmail.com

Abstract

"Education is not preparation for life; education is life itself. "The function of Education is to teach one to think intensively and to think critically. intelligence plus character- that is the goal of education" (Martin Luther King Jr).

Emotional intelligence is the ability to recognize, comprehend, and control our own and others emotions. It entails social and technical abilities that aid in efficient communication, sympathetic interactions and successful interpersonal relationships.

In Today's educational settings, emotional intelligence is linked to academic success. Students with greater emotional intelligence manage learning hurdles more efficiently and are more satisfied with their schooling. They are adaptable, collaborative, and resilient.

Emotional intelligence (EI) and values are interconnected concepts that foster holistic development in individuals. According to Daniel Goleman's seminal book, "Emotional Intelligence" (1995), EI encompasses self-awareness, self-regulation, motivation, empathy, and social skills.

Educators can integrate EI and values into teaching practices through strategies such as mindfulness, role-modeling, and service-learning projects. As noted by Linda Lantieri and Daniel Goleman in "Teaching Emotional Intelligence" (2008), these approaches promote a supportive learning environment.

By incorporating EI and values into teaching practices, educators can cultivate emotionally intelligent, socially responsible, and morally conscious individuals.

Multimedia Resource Management (MRM) Programme – Digital Repository for Teachers'

Jagadevi Nandikol

Research Scholar, Department of Education, Karnataka State Akkamahadevi WomenmUniversity, Vijayapur, Karnataka, India, Email: jagadvinandikol@gmail.com

Dr. Prakash. K. Badiger

Research Guide, DOE, KSAW University, Vijayapur, Karnataka & Associate Professor, CIET, NCERT, New Delhi – 110016, India, Email:

Abstract

This paper focuses on some major topic related to Multimedia resource management programme – digital repository for teachers. The rapid advancement of technology is reshaping the future of education, with MRM programs playing a pivotal role in this transformation. This paper explores the significance of MRM systems as digital repositories for teachers, providing centralized access to high quality multimedia resources that enhance teaching and learning experience. In the educational context, an MRM program helps teachers find, curate and integrate multimedia content into their lessons, improving engagement and learning outcome. These programs enable educators to enhance lesson planning and delivery through interactive and diverse media formats, fostering creativity and engagement in classroom. As education moves towards a more digital future, MRM systems will emerge as key factor for teachers in enhancing learning outcome. It act as an effective digital repository for teachers. Benefits of digital repositories for teachers is also been described in this paper. Furthermore, this paper focuses on key features of an effective MRM programs, such as search tools, multimedia integration and user friendly interfaces and highlight the benefits for teachers, including time efficiency, access to updated content and improved teaching method. Integrating multimedia resources in education sector enhances learning experiences. Teachers should be well equipped in using multimedia resource in teaching- learning process. MRM program provide a good platform for teachers to manage multimedia resources like video, image and audio which allows educators to create engaging and personalized lessons while fostering collaboration across educational institution. Furthermore, the challenges of unequal access to digital tools and potential solution are also discussed in this paper. The article concludes by emphasizing the transformative role MRM programs will play in shaping the future of education, empowering teachers, and enhancing student outcomes.

A Comparative Study of Social Intelligence, Emotional Intelligence and Self-Concept of B.Ed., Teacher Trainees of Mangaluru and Chikmagaluru District

Dr. Vijayalakshmi Naik,
Associate Professor, Institute of Education, Srinivas University, Mangaluru,
Email: vijayalakshmi498@gmail.com

Mrs. Mallika,
Research Scholar, Institute of Education, Srinivas University, Mangaluru,
Email: mallika.shetty365@gmail.com

Abstract

The present research deals with the 'A Comparative study of Social Intelligence, Emotional Intelligence and self-concept of B.Ed., teacher trainees of Mangaluru and Chikmagaluru district'. A total of 200 teacher trainees were randomly selected from two unaided institutions from Mangalore and one aided institution from Chikmagaluru district in Karnataka. They were administered three standardized tools to collect the data, they were a) Social Intelligence scale standardized by Dr. N.K.Chadha and Ms Usha Ganeshan (1986); b) Emotional Intelligence questionnaire standardized by Daniel Goleman; and c) Self-concept questionnaire standardized by Dr. Rajkumar Saraswat (1996). To assess the objectives of the study mean, median, Standard Deviation, 't' test and Pearson's co-efficient of correlation 'r' were employed. The present study shows that i) Majority of B.Ed., teacher trainees exhibited Social Intelligence (68.5%), Emotional Intelligence (72.5%) and Self-concept (70%) at Average level. ii) B.Ed., teacher trainees of Mangaluru and Chikmagaluru district do not differ in their Social Intelligence, Emotional Intelligence and Self-concept; iii) There was no relationship found among Social Intelligence, Emotional Intelligence and Self-concept of B.Ed., teacher trainees of Mangaluru and Chikmagaluru district. Educational implications: In the teacher education curriculum, theory as well as practical part of Social Intelligence, Emotional Intelligence and Self-concept are to be included, to become an effective teacher.

Educational Adjustment among Pre-University Students

Dr. Surma S

Assistant Professor, DOS&R in Psychology, Karnataka State Open University, Mysuru, Karnataka State, India. Email: surmapsy@gmail.com

Dr. Manjunatha P

Assistant Professor, DOS&R in Psychology, Karnataka State Open University, Mysuru, Karnataka State, India. Email: manjupsy2010@gmail.com

Vidya. M.

Research Scholar, Department of Studies& Research in Psychology, Karnataka State Open University, Mysuru, Karnataka State, India, Email: vidyaa.rcnv2022@gmail.com

Abstract

Educational adjustment is most important in the student's academic life. The purpose of this research is to assess the educational adjustment among Pre-University students. The   sample size of this research involves 240 Pre-University students, comprising 120 boys (60 Urban and 60 Rural) and 120 girls (60 Urban and 60 Rural) from various Pre-University Colleges in Bangalore. The standardized tool Adjustment Inventory developed by Dr. Penny Jain was employed for data collection. The obtained data were scored and was analysed using SPSS. The results revealed that there is a significant mean difference between boys and girls of Pre Univeristy Students on the level of educational adjustment. Girls have obtained a greater mean score (M=7.08, SD=1.82) on a total score of educational adjustment compared to boys (M=6.98, SD=2.06). It indicates that girls have shown a better level of educational adjustment compared to boys. This study contributes to the understanding of Educational adjustment among Pre-University students, providing insights into the importance of educational adjustment for effective academic achievement in student's life.

Assessment of Self-Identity among B.Ed. Students

Dr. Manjunatha P

Assistant Professor, DOS&R in Psychology, Karnataka State Open University, Mysuru, Karnataka State, India. Email: manjupsy2010@gmail.com

Dr. Surma S

Assistant Professor, DOS&R in Psychology, Karnataka State Open University, Mysuru, Karnataka State, India. Email: surmapsy@gmail.com

Devaraja A

Research Scholar, PG Department of Studies in Education, Karnataka University, Dharwad, Karnataka, India. Email: adevaraja1@gmail.com

Abstract

Self-identity is an individual's sense of who they are and it is the combination of their personality, physical attributes and interests. Self-identity for B.Ed students plays an important role as it influences how they teach, interact with students and create a learning environment. The aim of the present study was to assess the self-identity among B. Ed students. A descriptive survey design was employed, the sample size of this study consists of 160 B. Ed students, comprising 80 urban B. Ed students (40 Male & 40 Female) and 80 rural B.Ed students(40 Male & 40 Female) in Dharwad, Karnataka State by using a standardized Self understanding questionnaire for assessment. The SPSS version was used for data analysis. The results indicated that there is no significance difference between level of self-identity among male and female, urban and rural B. Ed Students. Male and female B. Ed students do not differ much on Self Identity. Rural B. Ed students have slightly better Self Identity than Urban B. Ed students. This study contributes to the understanding of self-identity in teacher educators and also develop intervention programmes.

Augmented Reality Pedagogy - A New Window in Science Teaching Learning

Saraswati D Bellundagi

Research Scholar, Department of Education, Karnataka State Akkamahadevi Women University, Vijayapura, Karnataka, India, Email: bellundagisaraswati@gmail.com

Dr. Prakash K Badiger

Research Guide, DOE, KSAW University, Vijayapura, Karnataka & Associate Professor, CIET, NCERT, New-Delhi, India

Abstract

Augmented Reality (AR) is emerging as a transformative pedagogical tool in science education, offering immersive and interactive experiences that enhance learning outcomes. This article explores the integration of AR in science curricula, highlighting its potential to foster engagement, facilitate complex concept visualization, and support diverse learning styles. Through case studies and empirical research, we illustrate how AR applications promote active learning, critical thinking, and collaborative problem-solving. The findings suggest that AR not only enriches the educational landscape but also prepares students for a technology-driven future, making science more accessible and engaging. Recommendations for educators and policymakers on effective AR implementation in science classrooms are provided.

Reflective Practice in Teaching

Manju J.
Assistant Professor, SKMK College of Education, Mysore,
Email- manjushreya33@gmail.com

Abstract

Reflective practice in teaching involves intentionally examining and analyzing one's teaching methods, strategies, and experiences to improve student learning outcomes and professional growth. Here are key aspects and benefits:

Benefits of Reflective practice: Reflective practice offers a range of benefits for personal and professional development. It helps individuals gain deeper self-awareness, enabling them to recognize their strengths, weaknesses and areas for improvement by reflecting on past experiences, professionals can avoid repeating mistakes and refine their approaches.

Models of Reflecting practice: Several models guide the process of reflecting practice. They are kolb's experiential learning cycle-emphasizing learning through experience and reflection by moving through four stages-concrete experience, Reflective observation, Abstract conceptualization, Active experimentation.

Gibb's reflecting cycle-commonly used model consisting of six stages: description, feelings, evaluation, analysis, conclusion and action plan. Schon's Reflection in action and reflection on action, which distinguishes between reflective during an experience and after it.

Strategies for Reflective Practice: To engage in effective reflective practice, individuals can use several strategies. Regular journaling is a popular approach, where individuals document their experiences, thoughts and feelings, then revisit them to identify pattern and areas of growth "what went well?" or What could have been differently?" can guide deeper reflection, whether after specific events or periodically, ensures it is come a consistent has it.

Competency-Based Education: Why Teacher's Professional Development Matters

Dr. M. Ponnambaleswari
Research Guide & Assistant Professor RV Teachers College, Bangalore,
Email: ponnamba@gmail.com

Roshna Joseph
Research Scholar, RV Teachers College & Assistant Professor,
Mount Carmel College, Bangalore. Email: helloroshna2@gmail.com

Abstract

The National Education Policy (NEP) 2020 introduced competency-based education (CBE) as a student-centric approach to teaching and learning in India. Competency-based education (CBE) is an approach to curriculum design, teaching – learning and evaluation that emphasizes on attainment of learning outcomes, in particular competencies in each subject. CBE methodology works to empower students and provide them with a meaningful and positive learning experience. It is a student-centered approach and actively engages them in the learning process. It emphasizes real-world applications of knowledge and skills and competencies. It is beyond the traditional method of simply relaying the teaching content, completing the syllabus, or conducting tests. In fact, it focuses on measuring the skills, knowledge, attitude, and competencies that the students attain at the end of schooling. Teachers and students who have been accustomed to conventional or traditional methods of teaching and learning may face issues. They might find the OBE model a little too modern, making them resist adopting it. This paper studied the challenges faced by the school science teachers in implementing the CBE based teaching practices in secondary schools. It also emphasizes the need of continuous professional development of teachers for the implementation of CBE at grass root levels.

Students Perception about New Education Policy-2020: A Study in Dakshina Kannada District

Dr.Ravikala
Assistant Professor in Commerce, Department of Commerce, Vivekananda College of Arts, Science and Commerce (Autonomous), Puttur. Dakshina Kannada, Karnataka
Email: ravikala77@gmail.com

Abstract

The National Education Policy (NEP) 2020 is a comprehensive agenda that aims to transform the Indian education system to meet the challenges of the 21st century. It introduces several innovative approaches to enhance the quality and inclusivity of education. According to the policy makers, NEP 2020 emphasizes the development of student's intellectual, creative, and social skills. The multidisciplinary nature of the curriculum would encourage students to explore a range of subjects. Students will have the flexibility to pick subjects across different streams as per their interests and career goals. This would break the rigid walls of subject-stream limitations and encourage cross-disciplinary learning. The study aims to understand the level of awareness, perception, and engagement of students, who are the stakeholders in these respective groups with the NEP 2020. Primary data was collected from 120 undergraduate students of Dakshina Kannada district by using a questionnaire in Google forms &

analysis was done through basic percentage analysis. To test the hypothesis chi square test was used. The findings provide insights into the awareness gaps and varying levels of engagement across the different educational levels, offering valuable implications for policymakers and educators to effectively implement the NEP 2020 reforms at each stage of education.

Impact of Mobile App Learning on Secondary School Students

Dr. Sushma R.
Assistant Professor, Department of Education, Rani Channamma University, Belagavi, Email: Email: sushmarcueducation@gmail.com

Kiran Vishwamber Rane
Research Scholar, Department of Education, Rani Channamma University, Belagavi, Email: kiranrane862@gmail.com

Abstract

Mobile learning apps have become more common among secondary school students. Mobile App learning provides new opportunities to learn outside of the traditional classroom. . As mobile technology becomes increasingly integrated into everyday life, educational apps are changing the way students study and engage with content. The questionnaire was provided to secondary school students to analyze their usage habits, experiences, and perceptions of mobile learning applications. According to the findings Of the study, mobile apps help students stay engaged, learn independently, and access educational resources at any time and from any location. This article analyses how Mobile Learning apps influence students' academic achievement, motivation, and study habits .While these tools improve learning outcomes for many students, issues such as excessive screen time and disparities in accessibility persist. Overall, mobile learning apps have a good impact on secondary school education; still, careful preparation is required to ensure they are used properly in schools.

A Study on Language Writing Skills of Secondary School Students

Dr P B Kavyakishore
Assistant Professor, Research Centre in Education, P G Dept of Education
R V Teachers College-IASE, Bengaluru, Email: drpbkkishore@gmail.com

Suvarnalata
Research Scholar, Research Centre in Education, P G Dept of Education
R V Teachers College-IASE, Bengaluru, Email: suvarnalata06mk@gmail.com

Abstract

Communication is one of the most essential requirements an individual needs to possess. A child learns to communicate verbally in the language to which it is exposed. Use of the language by the child leads to development of language skills. Development of language writing skill can be nurtured as it requires proper grammatical use with appropriate vocabulary. 'Writing is an activity that can improve students' vocabulary, grammatical structure, and idiom' Hossain(2015).

Language Education and Literacy is the basic need that has to be developed in the students by the teacher. Development of language be it any Indian language or foreign leads to the development of a child's cognitive abilities which helps the child to face the future challenges that are essential in today's technological and competitive world. This study is an attempt to know about the English language writing skills with the improvement of subskills such as Content, Organisation, Grammar, Vocabulary and Mechanics. The study was conducted on Karnataka State syllabus students where English is taken as second language. Study is conducted in Bangalore for both Urban-Rural on Kannada- English medium students.

Four schools were selected in Bangalore randomly and 190 students were chosen. Analysed the data based on descriptive statistics. To know the significant differences in language writing skills in relation to gender, locality and medium of instruction of secondary school students, t-test is used and was administered on the clusters of students that are Boys-Girls, Urban-Rural, Kannada-English medium students of Karnataka State syllabus with second language English.

The study on language writing skills of secondary school students concluded that based on the obtained mean scores, the girl students have good writing skills as compared to boys and English medium students have good writing skills as compared to Kannada medium students. The Urban and Rural students have average writing skills. The study prompts us to proceed with the activities for the improvement in the language writing skills (Content, Organisation, Grammar, Vocabulary and Mechanics) of secondary school students.

Digital Education Opportunities and Challenges

Dr.Nagaraja S H
Principal, Ramalingeshwara College of Education, Haranahalli – Kengapura,
Davanagere, Karnataka, Email:nagarajash68@gmail.com

Abstract

Digital education is largely an innovation of the last few decades, although it already existed in various forms slightly earlier. Shortly, the educational system environments are anticipated as mitigation to unforeseen natural and artificial pandemics such as Covid-19 in 2020 by the significant changes associated with the digitalization of some portion of the system. This article aims to provide valuable perspectives of ICT and digital education into its future benefits, risks, and challenges of embracing the latest technologies in the digital era, and vast online open courses. We have checked a profound change in the way we interact and generate within the academics with the advent of internet technologies. Globally, the digital revolution favoured open access to information. Classrooms today have a lot of ICT resources nearly all the teachers have made great strides to incorporate digital technology to increase access to information and collaborative activities for the learners.

Utilisation Level of Open Educational Resources (OER) among Teacher Educators

Balachandra Madiwal

Research Scholar, Department of Education Kuvempu University, Jnana Sahyadri, Shankaragatta, India, Email: balachandramadiwal@gmail.com

Dr. Patil S S

Professor, Department of Education Kuvempu University, Jnana Sahyadri Shankaragatta, India.

Abstract

The term Open Educational Resources (OER) was first introduced at UNESCO's 2002 Forum on Open Courseware and defined as "learning, teaching, and research materials in any format and medium that reside in the public domain or are under copyright but have been released under an open license that permits no-cost access, reuse, repurpose, adaptation, and redistribution by others" (UNESCO, 2019). OER has been shown to reduce learning costs, increase accessibility to educational resources, and enhance learning quality. The 5Rs of using OER (retain, reuse, revise, remix, and redistribute) can support innovation in teaching and learning).

The Open e-Learning Content Observatory Services (OLCOS) operates under the European eLearning Programme and is committed to advancing the creation, sharing, and global utilization of Open Educational Resources (OER). In 2007, OLCOS conducted a roadmap study that emphasized integrating innovative teaching methods with OER.

Over the last ten years, educators worldwide have been exploring using open educational resources (OER) in the teaching and learning process. There has been ongoing discussion among teachers about its terminology, benefits, and limitations. OER refers to technology-enabled educational resources that are openly provided and can be accessed and adapted for non-commercial use. It's important to distinguish OER from open learning, resource-based learning, or open publishing. OER takes advantage of new technology, allowing the incorporation of various media. According to Butcher

(2011, p.6), OER specifically refers to materials for teaching and learning that can be used for pedagogic purposes, including scholarly articles and content.

The Paris OER Declaration (UNESCO, 2012) defines open educational resources as "teaching, learning, and research materials in any medium, digital or otherwise, that reside in the public domain or have been released under an open license that permits no-cost access, use, adaptation, and redistribution by others with no or limited restrictions." This definition encompasses materials for undergraduate (UG), postgraduate (PG), and up to research and post-doctoral programs in higher education. Information and Communication Technology (ICT) plays a significant role, in shaping the traditional world in the context of globalization. Thanks to Open Educational Resources (OER), knowledge can be obtained at no cost.

This paper focuses on the study of the utilisation of OERs by the teacher educators of secondary educational institutions (B.Ed. Colleges) situated at an urban level under the Kuvempu University & Davangere University jurisdictions respectively. The sample consisted of 23 teacher educators at the urban level, and the survey method was used to collect the data. It was found that the level of utilisation towards open educational resources is found to be significantly moderate among secondary education teacher educators' awareness, and attitude in all streams.

Social Media a New Paradigm: Honing to Quality of Secondary Education

Shilpa N
Research Scholar, Department of Education Kuvempu University, Jnana Sahyadri Shankaragatta, Karnataka, Email: shilpayashvanth@gmail.com

Dr. Patil S S
Professor, Department of Education Kuvempu University, Jnana Sahyadri Shankaragatta, Karnataka

Abstract

A rapid change and development are observed in both software and hardware due to the innovative nature of computer and internet technologies. Social media is one of these. Social media is a wide definition of various network tools and technologies that emphasize the social characteristics of the internet as the communication and cooperation instrument of the 21st century, resulting from the developments in internet technologies. Although social media, which is a rapidly improving field, dates back to 1969 when CompuServe was used as an online service (Banks, 2007), . At the end of the 1990s, people began sharing messages, photos, and videos through their own blogs. Along with the increase in the usage degree that occurred as a result of the establishment of Facebook in 2004, YouTube in 2005, SlideShare, and Twitter in 2006, it was observed that social media settings, which served for various fields, were improved (Boyd and Ellison, 2008; Dao, 2015; Grosseck and Hotescu, 2008).

Social media has significantly impacted teenagers, especially at the secondary level. It provides virtual platforms for sharing information and ideas, including Facebook, YouTube, Telegram, Instagram, and WhatsApp. The effectiveness academic performance involves in recent days the continuous development of skills based on learnability and usage of social media technology.

The article discusses how social media platforms like Facebook, WhatsApp, Twitter, and YouTube impact students' academic performance. It emphasizes the crucial role of teachers in integrating technology effectively and the benefits of social media for blended learning. In recent years, secondary educational institutions, especially CBSE and ICSE schools, have embraced technology, offering students extensive opportunities to use it in their daily classroom activities and school administration. However, the successful integration of technology depends on it being a regular, transparent, and accessible practice that assists students in achieving their goals and reduces the burdens of both students and teachers.

Digital Literacy and Critical Thinking: Enhancing Student Learning

Dr. Hemanth Kumar B C
Assistant Professor, Shankaragowda College of Education, Mandya,
Email: bchemanth2010@gmail.com

Abstract

In the 21st century, digital literacy has emerged as a fundamental skill for students, extending far beyond traditional academic boundaries. As technology increasingly permeates all facets of life, the ability to effectively navigate, understand, and utilize digital platforms has become essential for communication, collaboration, and active participation in today's global economy. This paper explores the interconnectedness of digital literacy and critical thinking, highlighting their combined impact on student learning. Digital literacy equips students with the technical and cognitive skills required to assess, interpret, and engage with digital content, while critical thinking enables them to evaluate the credibility and relevance of the information they encounter. Together, these competencies foster improved problem-solving, creativity, and decision-making skills. The paper also addresses the challenges, such as the digital divide and information overload that hinder the development of these skills. Additionally, it offers strategies for integrating digital literacy and critical thinking into educational curricula, ultimately preparing students to thrive in a dynamic, technology-driven world. By fostering these essential skills, educators can equip students to become informed, responsible digital citizens, capable of navigating and contributing thoughtfully to the ever-changing digital landscape.

Lifelong Learning

Dr Manjunath H M
Assistant Professor, Sarada Vilas Teachers College, Mysore,
E-Mail: manjunathjasmin@gmail.com

Abstract

Lifelong learning is an ongoing process of acquiring knowledge, skills, and competencies throughout one's life. In today's fast-changing world, it is crucial for individuals to continuously learn and adapt to remain relevant in both personal and professional spheres. Lifelong learning encompasses formal, non-formal, and informal education, empowering people to keep pace with advancements in technology and shifts in the job market. It enhances personal growth by fostering creativity, curiosity, and cognitive health, while professionally, it equips individuals with the skills necessary to thrive in dynamic industries.

This continuous learning process also contributes to societal development by cultivating informed, engaged citizens capable of addressing complex global challenges such as climate change and inequality. However, barriers such as the digital divide, financial constraints, and time limitations hinder access to lifelong learning for many.

To promote inclusive learning, collaborative efforts among governments, educational institutions, and the private sector are essential. In Karnataka, initiatives like Kaushalya Karnataka and Sakshara Bharat Mission provide vocational training and literacy programs to support lifelong learning for all, particularly marginalized communities. These programs emphasize skill development, accessibility, and social equity, creating opportunities for individuals to enhance their employability and quality of life.

Ultimately, lifelong learning is key to personal fulfillment, professional success, and societal progress. By embracing continuous education, individuals and societies can foster adaptability, resilience, and a commitment to ongoing growth in an ever-evolving world.

E-Learning Platforms: An Innovation in Teaching and Learning

Smt. Asha M V
Lecturer, Minority Morarji Desai Residential College, Udugani,
Shikaripura, Shivamogga Dist, Email: ashamv1986@gmail.com

Abstract

Education has the ability to completely transform a Students life, as is well known. Learning modifies perception and thought processes. As a result of education and learning, you frequently challenge pre-existing assumptions. The purpose of education is to help Student and teacher think more critically and to help them form perspectives and views about life. It can help you become more intelligent and respected by others. A teacher with a wealth of ideas is able to explore of subjects, including the environment, and society. Education-based knowledge can be very helpful in guiding you towards the proper choices and decisions. Several Studies have been conducted so far in the field of Education with respect to the help with between E-Learning and an innovation in teaching.

And Learning

E-Learning Platforms is a new and innovative Teaching and Learning to enhance the teaching and learning process. This Platform is widely used in schools as well as colleges and universities. This Platform facilitates the teacher and the learner to interact in the dual mode system i.e., online and face-to face mode. This paper highlighted the concept of Online Platform, role of learner in the E-Learning, apps and mode of E-Learning platforms. Features of online learning, effectiveness of innovation of for teacher and learner. The variety of strategies for resource description taken by these platforms is also discussed. These range from formal machine-readable metadata to human readable text. It is related that resource description should be seen as a purely technical activity.

A Quantitative Analysis of Educational Developments and Economic Growth of Indian Economy

Rohit DSilva
Lecturer in Economics, Dept. Of Economics, S D M Degree College Honnavar,
Email: dsilvarohit33@gmail.com

Abstract

"There is no better investment a nation can make than education. It is an investment in economic development, an investment in opportunity and an investment in our shared future." - Evelin Weber

Under the context of Globalisation, education is playing vital role in the development of an economy and economic development lies on the growth of GNP/GDP. Modern education requires adequate and effective investment of Educational resources. The main objective of this study is to indicate the contribution of modern education evolving levels of economic progress in globalised Economy, i.e. Indian Economy. This is not only the attempt to measure the contribution of education to growth but also examines educational structure corresponding to modern world. Gross National Product, as an annual rate of growth and per capita is used as the best measure of economic progress. Budget allocation, Educational Expenditure, School enrollment, Student-teacher ratio parameters are used to measure the growth of education in India. The study covers the comparison of trends in the distribution of expenditure by level of governments and by levels of school. The study suggests to overview the public expenditure on modern education.

Digital Assessment Tools for Peer and Self-Assessment

Beeralingaiah. G
Assistant Professor, Shankaragowda College of Education, Mandya,
Email: beeal1026@gmail.com
Dr. Krishnappa. N
Assistant Professor, Department of Education, Karnataka State Open University,
Mysore, Email: krishn_n@rediffmail.com

Abstract

In the evolving educational landscape, peer and self-assessment have become essential components of student-centered learning. These assessment methods foster deeper engagement, critical thinking, and self-reflection by encouraging students to take active roles in evaluating both their own work and that of their peers. The integration of digital tools such as Peergrade, Google Classroom, Flipgrid, and Moodle has revolutionized peer and self-assessment, making them more scalable, interactive, and efficient. These platforms provide instant, formative feedback, empowering students to reflect on their learning, set personalized goals, and gain diverse perspectives through peer review. Moreover, the use of these digital tools supports collaborative learning, enhancing communication and engagement among students. Despite the numerous benefits, challenges such as technological barriers, bias in assessments, and data privacy concerns persist. This paper explores the advantages of digital tools in peer and self-assessment, including increased student accountability, improved learning outcomes, and the promotion of reflective practice. Additionally, it addresses the need for training educators and students to effectively use these tools while maintaining the validity and reliability of assessments. Ultimately, the integration of digital assessment tools enhances student learning by fostering a collaborative and reflective learning environment that is key to modern education.

Artificial Intelligence: Perception of Student Teachers

Dr. Manju N. D
Assistant Professor, National College of Education, Shimoga,
Email: manjundphd@gmail.com

Abstract

The research study was undertaken to investigate the perception of Pre-service teachers towards Artificial intelligence. The sample of 100 Pre-service teachers (B. Ed Student Teachers) from Shimoga city was selected by adopting Stratified random sampling technique based on the independent variables namely Gender and Stream. Pre-Service teachers Perception towards Artificial intelligence was accessed with the help of the Perception towards Artificial intelligence Scale constructed by the investigator Dr. Manju N. D. Specific objectives formulated were: 1. To assess the level of perception of Pre-service teachers towards Artificial Intelligence. 2. To find whether there is any significant difference between male and female teachers with respect to their perception towards Artificial Intelligence. 3. To find whether there is any significant difference between Arts and Science Stream Pre-service teachers with respect to their perception towards Artificial intelligence. Descriptive survey method was adopted for the study. The data obtained from the survey was analyzed by using Percentage analysis and t-test. Findings of the study were: 1. More than half of the pre-service teachers in Shimoga city i.e., 60.0% of them possess an Average perception towards Artificial Intelligence and 35% possess highly favourable perception in Artificial Intelligence, and only 5% of the pre-service teachers possess less perception towards Artificial intelligence. 2. There is no significant difference between male and female pre-service teachers in their perception towards Artificial Intelligence.3. There is no significant difference between Arts and Science Pre-serviced teachers in their perception towards Artificial Intelligence.

STEAM Education

Poornima T M
Assistant Professor, KSSM B.Ed College. Shivamogga,
Email: proonimatm73@gmail.com

Abstract

STEAM education refers to an interdisciplinary approach to learning that integrates the fields of Science, Technology, Engineering, and Mathematics. The goal is to develop critical thinking, problem-solving, and collaboration skills through hands-on projects and real-world applications.

The objectives of STEAM education include developing critical thinking and problem-solving skills, fostering collaboration and teamwork, promoting interdisciplinary learning, providing hands-on experience, ensuring technological proficiency, preparing students for future careers in high-demand fields, instilling a passion for lifelong learning, and promoting equity and inclusion in access to STEAM opportunities.

STEAM education promotes a more integrated curriculum that enhances the multifaceted talents and skills of students. Unlike the old STEAM curriculum, the focus of STEAM is now more on practical skills, including social, emotional, and communication skills

In conclusion, STEAM education is essential for preparing students to navigate the complexities of the modern world. By integrating science, technology, engineering, and mathematics, it fosters critical thinking, creativity, and collaboration. This foundation equips learners to tackle real-world challenges, driving innovation and economic progress while empowering individuals to contribute meaningfully to society and addressing global issues.

Effectiveness of Kolb's experiential learning model on communication Among 9th grade (CBSE) Students

Santhosh Albert Saldanha
Principal, SDM College of Education, Ujire.
Email: santhosh.saldanha@gmail.com

Abstract

Kolb's experiential learning model in language could be learner-centred and enhance communication by the implementation of Kolb's experiential learning model. In Kolb's experiential learning model students play an active role and learn to reflect on their learning experiences. In the present study, the researcher has reviewed prior studies and formulated hypothesis. The experimental method was adopted for students from the CBSE board and English as the medium of instruction. The 35 students were taught using the conventional method of teaching and 35 students were taught using Kolb's experiential learning model. The instructional module prepared for the topic of THE BOND OF LOVE (English Prose). The Kolb's experiential learning model includes Stage 1: Experiencing (concrete experience), Stage 2: Examining (Reflective observation), Stage 3: Explaining (abstract conceptualization), 4. Concrete Experience, Stage 5: (Active Experimentation) The Pre-test was conducted before the implementation of the program and the post-test was administered after the program. Data were analysed by applying the Anova and the hypotheses were tested. The study revealed that the experimental group has performed better in the communication as compared to the control group. Kolb's experiential learning model in language increases communication among the learners. The instructional program based on Kolb's experiential learning model activities increases communication.

The study recommends that, such learning can be imparted in different curriculum and also for different age groups of students.

Future Skills and Competencies in Education: Preparing Learners for the Next Generation

Dr. Dhanyakumar G K,
Assistant Professor, Sri BGS B.Ed College, Sringeri,
Email: dk0danya@gmail.com

Amrutha V N
Assistant Professor, Sri BGS B.Ed College, Sringeri
Email: amruthahebbar2584@gmail.com

Abstract

In an era defined by rapid technological advancements, the future of education must pivot toward equipping learners with a new set of skills and competencies. This paper explores the critical future skills that will define successful learning outcomes, including digital literacy, critical thinking, problem-solving, emotional intelligence, creativity, and adaptability. By reviewing recent educational research and trends, this paper seeks to offer insight into how education systems can be redesigned to incorporate these skills into curricula. The discussion is informed by top academic works in the field, including foundational texts on 21st-century skills, cognitive psychology, and emerging pedagogies. The implications for policy, curriculum development, and teacher training are explored, with an emphasis on ensuring inclusivity and equity in future learning environments.

Introduction to Future Education

Dr. Nagesh K C
Principal, Sri BGS B.Ed College, Sringeri, Email: nageshkckalmane@gmail.com

Ramesh A C
Assistant Professor, Sri BGS B.Ed College, Sringeri, Email: rameshac225@gmail.com

Abstract

The whole concept of the future of education binds together the evolution of learning models, technology integration, and personalized approaches that shall eventually shape the learners for their survival in a rapidly changing world. Future education propped up by developments in artificial intelligence, virtual and augmented reality, and data-driven learning tools, would be flexible, inclusive, and even learner-cantered.

Personalised Learning Adaptive platforms of learning in the future will surge and build more on personalising education based on the needs of each individual student concerning learning style and speed. AI-enabled systems study performance data and make recommendations based on custom learning pathways for each learner. Integration of Technologies into Learning: This would cover virtual classrooms, VR/AR simulations, and AI tutors. Such technologies enable students to become immersed in the interaction of real-life scenarios and make learning much more interactive and effective. Lifelong Learning: As industries continue to change and upgrade, the need for the development of continuous skills will banditry. Students will get to have exposure to the best teachers and resources available across the globe, erasing all geographical boundaries. Emphasis on Crucial Skills: Future curricula will emphasize much more on critical-thinking skills, creativity, collaboration skills, and emotional intelligence than on rote memorization.

Effect of Theater-Based Teaching on Students' Achievement in Kannada Language among IX Standard Students

Pushpa R.
Research Scholar, P.G. Department of Studies in Education, Davanagere University, Shivagangothri, Davangere, Email ID: pushpalokesh79@gmail.com

Dr. Rangaswamy C.
Research Guide and Assistant Professor, P.G. Department of Studies in Education, Davanagere University, Shivagangothri, Davangere, Email:

Abstract

Theater-based education has come out as a active and attractive instructional type that fosters deeper education through active participation, creativity and emotional commitment. In the circumstance of language learning, mainly in Kannada, theater-based approaches provide authentic, culturally related experiences that help students extend better language comprehension, critical thinking as well as communication skills. This type of method is mainly important for nurturing a more overall understanding of the language, making it a valuable tool for improving academic achievement among school students. This study involved a sample of 40 ninth-grade students, separated into two groups: an experiment group (N=20) taught using theater-based method and a controlled group (N=20) taught using traditional method of teaching. The intervention included interactive theater exercises, role-playing activities as well as discussions centered on culturally relevant narratives. A 'Randomized Matching Control Group Pre-test Post-Test' research design was utilized, with the Achievement Test in Kannada Language-developed by the researcher and consisting of 40 multiple choice items used to assess students' achievement and the reliability of the test was confirmed through test-retest technique. The independent 't' test revealed that theater-based teaching was significantly more effective than traditional method in improving Kannada language achievement among ninth-grade students. Theater-based teaching not only enhances student learning but also fosters teachers' professional growth, positioning it as a key approach in determining creative, adaptive and effective educators for the future.

Best Practice of ADVS First Grade College Library Sasvehalli: A Study

Shankarappa N
Selection Grade Librarian, ADVS First Grade College,
Sasvehalli, Honali Taluk Davangere, Email: shankrappan18@gmail.com

Abstract

Best Practices is continuous process by adapting new technology in the library services and can be provided effectively. This study mainly focuses on various best practices adapted by ADVS First Grade College Library. Here are some traditional best practices: Information Technology (IT) based practices and general practices that academic libraries can adopt to enhance their services which are useful guide for other libraries.

Importance of Digital Library for Students

Sri. Basavaraja C
Librarian. Sri Venkateshwara College of Education, Near Chalkere Toll Gate, Chitradurga.

Abstract

During the past recent years, there has been tremendous development reaming the concept of digital libraries, the biggest online platform of knowledge that can be stored and retrieved through online networks. Digital libraries are considered as the most complex form of data systems that associate with the digital document preservation, distributed database management, hypertext, filtering, information retrieval, and selective dissemination of information. This has really overcome geographical barrier offering a wide range of academic, research, and cultural resources with multimedia effects which can be accessed around the world over the distributed networks. This article provides information to the audience on the subject matter in terms of what has been already discovered and explored on the importance of Digital Library and what all can be further explored. The literature pertaining to the studies relating to how digital libraries emerged discussed in this article. The idea is to brief the readers about the concept of library resources shifted into digital libraries with the help of technology and its growth sourced from already existing literature. The contemporary trends reflecting the current state of the library and how it has progressed over time also discussed here.

A Comparative Study of Social and Educational Adjustment of Male and Female Adolescence Students

Dr. Amitkumar Shankarrao Gagare
Associate Professor, SSB College of Education, Shrirampur, Dist – Ahmedngare, Maharashtra, Email: asgagare@gmail.com

Abstract

This paper attempts to understand and analyze the social and educational adjustment ability among adolescence in Satara City. Present study classify adjustment in two important Categories i.e. Social adjustment and emotional adjustment. The method used in the study was a survey. A Survey was taken on near about 475 (188 male & 287 Female) samples. The result reported that there were significant difference in Social and educational adjustment among adolescence.

The Use of Educational Apps and Mobile, in Learning of Visually Impaired People

Dr. S. Karthiyayeni
Principal, R.V Teachers College, Bengaluru, Email: karthiyayeni.rvtc@rvei.edu.in

Shashi. N
Research Scholar, R.V Teachers College, Bengaluru, Email: n.shashiravi@gmail.com

Abstract

Visual impairment is a disability that affects the eye function. Due to this reason that people have common barriers like low vision are complete blind. This impairment, make them to struggle in their learning and lead a comfortable life, even though they are overcoming of those obstacle by using educational apps and mobile devices. This research article will try to reveal how educational Apps and mobile devices useful in learning of visually impaired people. The participants rated use of educational apps and mobile devices for their learning activities and professional work. Researcher prepared the Google questionnaire and collected the data from visually impaired people. Collected data was analyzed with the statistical techniques. The questionnaire include educational apps and mobile devices which they use. This research study also try to get information of the accessibility of YouTube Whats-app, Instagram usage for their learning. Most of the visually impaired people depend on auditory learning so this study also try to focus on how this social media is helpful in visually impaired people learning activity and daily life.

Emerging Technologies for Best Learning Outcomes

Dr. Shashikala G. M.
Assistant Professor, M. M. College of Education, Davanagere, Karnataka.
Email skalagm@gmail.com

Dr. Savitha A.C.
Assistant Professor, Department of Electronics & Communication,
J.S.S. Academy of Technical Education, Bengaluru- India

Abstract

Technology is the more comprehensive backbone for various organizations. A smart education becomes a trend in education that meets sustainability objectives. Developments in Artificial Intelligence, Block Chain Technology, Cloud Computing, Machine Learning, M2M Communication, 5G/6G Networks, and other emerging technologies have transformed the traditional educational system into one that is more intelligent, interactive, and collaborative. New technologies have a big impact on blended learning, online learning, and offline learning. The innovative development of the Internet of Things has improved teacher-student communication and improved outcome-based learning. In the sphere of education, students employ modern technology to complete assignments. With the aid of 3-D models and videos, students can comprehend material and evaluate data. Artificial intelligence's usage in course design and student learning route recommendation. The goal of this research is to investigate the cutting edge technologies for outcome-based educational systems. Education is becoming into a ubiquitous, institutionalized, and intelligent process. The effectiveness and efficiency of smart education are increased by emerging technology.

Influence of Social Media on Academic Achievement of Secondary School Students

Dr. N Krishnappa
Assistant Professor, Dept of Education, KSOU, Mysore, Email: krishn_n@rediffmail.com

Ramajansab Allasab Waddatti
Research Scholar, Dept of Education, KSOU, Mysore, Email: nadafwaddatti@gmail.com

Abstract

The purpose of this research study is to examine the influence of Social Media on Academic Achievement of the students of the Secondary School Students of Gadag district. Students' academic performance is influenced by social factors. These factors include romantic relationships, student cults, membership in clubs and organizations, and sports. Sampling via mid-point square approach was used to compare social variables with the students' CGPA. Both the f-test at 0.05 level of significance and regression indicate that romantic relationships and student cults have a significant effect on academic performance, while club or organization activity and excessive sporting is not significant. Social media offers various educational benefits. It serves as a platform for sharing knowledge, ideas, and resources among students and educators. Social media communities and groups provide opportunities for collaborative learning, enabling students to discuss and explore academic topics beyond the classroom

Teacher-Educators and Student-Teachers Academic Relationship of Aided and Unaided Teacher-Education Institutions

Sandeepa L
Research Scholar, Department of PG Studies & Research in Education, Kuvempu University, Shankaraghatta, Shimoga, Email: sandeepl2508@gmail.com

Dr. Jagannath K. Dange.
Professor, Dean, Faculty of Education, & Chairman, Department of PG Studies & Research in Education, Kuvempu University, Shankaraghatta, Shimoga

Abstract

This study explores the dynamic relationship between teacher-educators and student-teachers in both aided and unaided teacher education institutions, with a focus on SC/ST, General, and Minority categories. Using a descriptive survey approach, the research investigates how academic relationships differ across these institutional contexts, emphasizing the role of mentorship, feedback, and collaborative engagement in pedagogical development, both inside and outside the classroom. The Teacher-Educators and Student-Teachers Academic Relationship Scale (TSAR), with a high reliability score (Cronbach's Alpha of 0.968), was employed to gather data. Through qualitative and quantitative analyses, the study examines how these interactions influence student teachers' self-efficacy, instructional skills, and classroom preparedness. The findings highlight the critical role of supportive and reflective relationships in enhancing student teachers' confidence and competence, ultimately improving the overall quality of education. Recommendations are provided to optimize teacher-educator and student-teacher interactions, fostering environments conducive to effective teaching and learning, tailored to the needs of diverse institutional settings.

Significance of Digital Tools and Techniques in Current Scenario

A H Gopal

Assistant professor, BGS College of Education, Adichunchanagiri University, Mandya,

Email: ahgopal64@gmail.com

Abstract

In the digital era, technology has revolutionized the way we work, learn, and interact. Digital tools and techniques have emerged as essential components of modern life, empowering individuals and organizations to achieve unparalleled levels of productivity, creativity, and success.

Digital tools and techniques refer to the software, hardware, and methodologies used to create, design, develop, and manage digital content, processes, and systems. These tools facilitate various tasks, from graphic design and web development to data analysis, marketing, and communication. Digital education is the innovative incorporation of modern technology and digital tools to assist the progress of teaching and learning. It is also known as Technology Enhanced Learning (TEL), digital learning, or e-learning. Digital education is the way forward to seeking education through the means of technology and digital devices.

The emergence of the internet and ever-evolving technology has made learning interactive, engaging, motivating, and handy. Education is not anymore limited to textbooks and classrooms; it has become an amalgamation of technology, innovative learning, and digital content. The internet has become far more affordable and accessible and this shall lead to a greater confluence of digital and traditional teaching methods. The government is actively involved in taking essential steps to come forward with policies that will boost the digital education market in India.

Digital tools and techniques have revolutionized the way we live, work, and interact. Understanding and leveraging these tools is crucial for digital tools and techniques have profoundly transformed the way we live, work, and interact, revolutionizing industries, and redefining productivity, creativity, and innovation. Embracing these tools is crucial for personal and professional growth, business success, and staying competitive in the digital landscape. By leveraging digital tools and techniques, individuals and organizations can unlock new opportunities, drive growth, and thrive in an increasingly digital world.

A Comprehensive Meta-Analysis of the Relationship between Flipped Learning with Academic Achievement

Dr. M Ponnambaleshwari,
Assistant Professor in Education, Department of P.G. Studies in Education & Research, R.V. Teachers College (IASE), Bangalore, Email: ponnamba@gmail.com

Raghu K S
Research Scholar, Department of P.G. Studies in Education & Research, R.V. Teachers College (IASE), Bangalore. Email: raghufrmblore@gmail.com

Abstract

"If we teach today as we taught yesterday, we rob our children of tomorrow." – John Dewey. Technological advancement has facilitated the learners to maximise the opportunity to attain knowledge and understanding. The flipped learning has gained the great attention of many researchers as a result of what teachers are implementing in their classrooms. Academic Achievement is the extent to which a student, teacher, or institution has attained their short or long-term educational goals. The main objective of the paper is to comprehend the relationship between flipped learning with academic achievement.

Several studies have been conducted so far in the field of Education with respect to the relationship between Flipped learning and academic achievement. Most of the studies have concluded a positive relationship between Flipped learning and academic achievement at different levels. The sole purpose of this study is to conduct a meta-analysis to provide a quantitative synthesis of research findings on the relationship between Flipped learning and Academic Achievement.

A Study on Causes and Consequences of School Dropouts in Vijayapura City

Dr. Prakash Sannakkanavar
Assistant Professor Research Guide, Department of Education, Karnataka Sate Akkamahadevi Women University, Vijayapura-586108, Email: drprakashedu84@gmail.com

Abstract:

Education has the ability to completely transform a person's life, as is well known. Learning modifies perception and thought processes. As a result of education and learning, you frequently challenge pre-existing assumptions. This distinction in instruction enables you to broaden your horizons and engage with people without bias. The purpose of education is to help people think more critically and to help them form perspectives and views about life. It can help you become more intelligent and respected by others. People in society come in varied shapes and have diverse perspectives. A person with a wealth of ideas is able to explore and debate a wide range of subjects, including politics, the environment, and society. Education-based knowledge can be very helpful in guiding you towards the proper choices and decisions.

Understanding and interpreting the wide range of complicated elements that contribute to the occurrence of students dropping out of school will be aim of this study. In particular, the phenomenon of high school dropouts is highlighted by this study. Numerous family, school, and community factors will be found in the research data to influence students' likelihood of graduating or dropping out of high school. These include: poverty, a lack of family and school stability, almost all of the participants' parents were dropouts themselves, social conduct, rebellion, peer pressure, and a sense of caring.

Enhance and Sustain Learning through Blended Approach

Laxmi Bellundagi D.,
Research scholar, P.G Department of Studies in Education, Karnatak University,
Dharwad, Email: laxmibellundagi05@gmail.com

Dr.N.S.Talawar,
Assistant Professor, Karnatak University College of Education,
Karnataka University, Dharwad

Abstract

This study investigates the effectiveness of a blended learning approach in Enhancing and sustaining student engagement and academic performance. By integrating online resources, interactive Multimedia and face to face instruction examines that how this hybrid mode can cater to divers learning styles and promote active participation. Data were collected through surveys and focus groups involving students and educators across multiple disciplines.

Findings reveal that students experienced increased motivation and improved learning outcomes, with 80% reporting a preference for the blended learning mode over traditional methods. The results suggest that blended learning not only enhances immediate understanding but also fosters a deeper, more sustained engagement with course material. This study underscores the potential of blended learning as a viable strategy for modern educational settings, providing insights for educators seeking to create more dynamic and effective learning environments. So that in this paper we are going to see that how it benefits for the students learning, professional development and outcomes of blended learning.

Impact of Social and Emotional Learning on Students' Well-Being

Dr. Raghavendra Bommannavar
Assistant Professor, PG Dept. of Education & Research R.V. Teachers College, Bengaluru.
E-mail: raghuedn@gmail.com

Dr. Mallikarjun B Kudavakkalagi
Assistant Professor & Principal, Sri Vivekananda College of Education, Arsikere, Hasana,
E-mail: mbkrie@gmail.com

Abstract

The cutting-edge teaching method known as social and emotional learning (SEL) develops students' social competencies, emotional intelligence, and self-regulation abilities while fostering overall development. The essential benefits of SEL on students' welfare—including their emotional, psychological, social, and academic well-being—are examined in this study. Social-emotional learning (SEL) directly enhances mental health, lowers stress levels, and increases resilience by teaching children how to control their emotions, form healthy relationships, and make wise decisions. Additionally, SEL enhances students' social skills, leading to stronger peer relationships and larger support systems—both essential for preserving emotional stability.

Studies show that students who participate in SEL programs have better academic results, lower anxiety, and higher self-esteem. SEL also fosters a supportive and nurturing school climate that enhances children's overall wellbeing. This abstract highlights the long-term advantages of incorporating SEL into the educational curriculum for improving student wellbeing and academic success, underscoring the crucial role that SEL plays in equipping students to confront life's difficulties with confidence and emotional stability

NEP 2020: Challenges and Opportunities in Future Education

Nataraju M S
Research Scholar, Dept of Studies & Research in Education, KSOU, Mysuru,
Email: msnataraju72@gmail.com

Abstract

The greatest instrument at our disposal for maximizing the interplay of democracy, diversity, and justice is education. In the absence of variety, democracy may be exclusive. Without democracy, diversity may be flimsy. Furthermore, justice cannot be attained without democracy and tolerance for differences. However, there's still much work to be done before education can fulfill its potential—the Challenges we face today and in the future call for teamwork. Governments by themselves are unable to resolve them. Rather, we must empower and inspire everyone to take part in bringing about change.

Unfortunately, education in the world today is unfit for these uses. Urgently needed is a fundamental overhaul of education. CAN YOU VISUALIZE TRANSFORMATION? Transformation refers to significant adjustments made to global educational offerings and procedures. This is not so much a total overturning. We shall require significantly different services from education than we have received in the past. However, a new approach must be taken to complete this transition, as compared to the past. More inclusive engagement and a stronger public discourse are required, focusing on those whose voices, cultures, and knowledge have been marginalized and excluded.

A Study on Teacher Self-Efficacy Among Teacher Educators

Prashanth N.S.
Assistant Professor, Department of Education, B.E.S.M. Arts and Commerce College, Bydagi - 581106
Karnataka, email: prashnthns1984@gmail.com

Abstract

The present study aims to examine the teacher self-efficacy among teacher educators. The investigator has adopted causal comparative method under descriptive method of research. The sample consists of 300 teacher educators from different colleges affiliated to Davangere University, Kuvempu University and Vijayanagara Sri Krishnadevaraya University through stratified random sampling technique. The investigator used the standardized tool to measure the teacher self-efficacy among teacher educators. To interpret the raw scores, data were analyzed using mean, standard deviation, and t-test. The finding shows that female teacher educators are having more self-efficacy scores compare male teacher educators. The unaided teacher educators have higher self-efficacy scores values compared to aided teacher educators. Further, the teaching experience does not have a significant impact on teacher self-efficacy scores among the teacher educators.

Reflective Pathways: Enhancing Self-Efficacy and Teacher Identity Through Self-Reflection in B.Ed. Programs

Prof. M.C.Yerriswamy
Professor, School of Education, Rani Channamma University, Belagavi.
Yogisha. S
Research Scholar, School of Education, Rani Channamma University, Belagavi

Abstract

This study explores the role of self-reflection in enhancing self-efficacy and shaping teacher identity among Bachelor of Education (B.Ed.) students. Through qualitative methods, including interviews and reflective journals, the research examines how structured self-reflection practices impact future educators' confidence and sense of professional identity. Findings suggest that regular engagement in self-reflection not only fosters greater self-awareness but also empowers students to navigate challenges and uncertainties in their teaching journey. The implications for B.Ed. programs highlight the necessity of integrating self-reflection as a core component of teacher education curricula, ultimately supporting the development of competent and resilient educators.

The Efficacy of Gamification and Mastery learning strategies in Geography performance of high school students

Ms. Pushpanjali Y
Research Scholar, Dept. of Studies in Education,   Vijayanagara Sri Krishnadevaraya University, Ballari, Email: pushpanjali12456@gmail.com

Dr. Sushma N Jogan
Research Supervisor, Dept. of studies in Education, Vijayanagara Sri Krishnadevaraya University, Ballari

Abstract

Currently, gamification learning practices can support sustainable development by expanding the audience for the knowledge provided by a certain nation or institution. Greater flexibility, autonomy, interaction, and more effective learning outcomes are made possible by mastery learning, which also presents a big opportunity to reorganize and change the high school curriculum. The study was quasi-experimental randomized Pretest-Posttest Control Group Design. It is the goal to investigate the differences in post-test mean scores between high school students who were taught using GLS, MLS, and conventional strategies. To achieve this, an experimental method was employed. The researcher has collected quantitative data from 90 students of high school through the Purposive sampling technique. The instrument used for data collection was Geography achievement test (GAT) standardized by the researcher. Analyses of the acquired data were conducted using ANOVA and the relevant t-Test. The findings reveal that the experimental group of high school students have performed better taught geography using gamification and mastery learning strategy.

ಕಾರಂತರು ಮತ್ತು ಗಾಂಧಿ ಶೈಕ್ಷಣಿಕ ಚಿಂತನೆಗಳು

ಡಾ. ಉಮೇಶ್ ಅಂಗಡಿ

ಸಹಾಯಕ ಪ್ರಾಧ್ಯಾಪಕರು, ಡಿ ವಿ ಎಸ್ ಕಲಾ ಮತ್ತು ವಿಜ್ಞಾನ ಕಾಲೇಜು. ಶಿವಮೊಗ್ಗ,

Email: umeshangadi@dvsdegreecollege.org

ಸಾರಾಂಶ

ಚರಿತ್ರೆ ಎನ್ನುವುದು ಕಳೆದು ಹೋದುದರ ಮರು ಪರಿಶೀಲನೆಯೂ ಹೌದು. ಇಲ್ಲಿ ಮರುಪರಿಶೀಲನೆ ಎನ್ನುವುದು ನ್ಯಾಯಬದ್ಧವಾಗಿರುತ್ತದೆ. ಅದರ ಜೊತೆಗೆ ಅದು ಶೈಕ್ಷಣಿಕವಾಗಿರುತ್ತದೆ. ಅದು ಅತ್ಯಂತ ಸಹಜವೂ ಆಗಿರುತ್ತದೆ. ಚರಿತ್ರೆಯನ್ನು ಇಂಗ್ಲಿಶಿನಲ್ಲಿ ಹಿಸ್ಟರಿ ಎಂದು ಕರೆಯುತ್ತೇವೆ. ಮೂಲ ಪದ ಗ್ರೀಕಿನದು. ಹಿಸ್ಟಾರಿಯಾ ಎಂದು ಗ್ರೀಕಿನಲ್ಲಿ ಬಳಸುತ್ತಾರೆ. ಹಾಗೆಂದರೆ ಪರಿಶೀಲನೆ ಮಾಡು ಎಂದು ಅರ್ಥ. ಸಂಶೋಧನೆಯ ಮೂಲಕ ಯಾವುದನ್ನು ನಾವು ಕಂಡುಕೊಳ್ಳುತ್ತೇವೆಯೋ ಅದು ಹಿಸ್ಟ್ರಿ ಆಗುತ್ತದೆ. ಜರ್ಮನಿಯ ಅತ್ಯಂತ ಸುಪ್ರಸಿದ್ಧ ಚರಿತ್ರೆಕಾರನು ಒಂದು ಮಾತನ್ನು ಹೇಳುತ್ತಾನೆ: "ನಿಜವಾಗಿಯೂ ಆಗಿರುವುದು ಏನು?" ಅವನು ವಾಸ್ತವಕ್ಕೆ ಹೆಚ್ಚಿನ ಮಹತ್ವವನ್ನು ಕೊಡುತ್ತಾನೆ. ಇದೇ ಪ್ರಶ್ನೆ ಈ ಕಾವ್ಯದಲ್ಲಿದೆ. ಆಧುನಿಕ ಜಾತ್ಯಾತೀತವಾದ, ವೈಜ್ಞಾನಿಕ ಮನೋಸ್ಥಿತಿಯು ಹೇಗೆ ಕೆಲಸವನ್ನು ಮಾಡುತ್ತದೆ ಎನ್ನುವುದನ್ನು ನಾವು ಅವನ ಬರಹಗಳಲ್ಲಿ ಕಾಣಬಹುದು ಎಂದು ವಿಮರ್ಶಕರು ಅಭಿಪ್ರಾಯಪಡುತ್ತಾರೆ. ಅವನ ವಿಶಿಷ್ಟತೆಯೆಂದರೆ ಇತಿಹಾಸವನ್ನು ಅವನು ತತ್ವಜ್ಞಾನದ ಬೆಳಕಿನಲ್ಲಿ ನೋಡಿರುವುದು. ಚರಿತ್ರೆಯ ಮಾತ್ರವೇ ಸತ್ಯವನ್ನು ಹೇಳುತ್ತದೆ ಎಂಬ ವಾದವನ್ನು ಅವನು ನಿರಾಕರಿಸುತ್ತಾನೆ. ಚರಿತ್ರೆಯ ಅಧ್ಯಯನಕ್ಕೆ ವಾಸ್ತವವಾಗಿ ವಿಜ್ಞಾನದ ಬೆಂಬಲವು ಬೇಕು ಎನ್ನುವುದು ಅವನ ನಿಲುವು. ಚರಿತ್ರೆಯಲ್ಲಿ ಒಂದು ಘಟನೆ ಮತ್ತು ಒಂದು ನಿರ್ಣಯ ಎನ್ನುವುದು ಇರಲು ಸಾಧ್ಯವಿಲ್ಲ. ಒಂದು ಕಥನಕ್ಕೆ ಹೇಗೆ ಹಲವು ಸಾಧ್ಯತೆಗಳು ಇರುತ್ತವೆಯೋ ಅದೇ ರೀತಿಯಲ್ಲಿ ಒಂದು ಚಾರಿತ್ರಿಕ ಸಂಗತಿಯಲ್ಲಿ ಅನೇಕ ವಾದ ವಿವಾದಗಳು ಇರುತ್ತವೆ.

ಅದರ ಫಲವಾದ ಸಾಮಾಜಿಕ ರೀತಿ–ನೀತಿಗಳು ಇನ್ನೂ ಅಳಿದಿರಲಿಲ್ಲ (ಗ್ರಾಮಾಯಣ, ಭಾಗ–1). ಈ ಕಾದಂಬರಿಯಲ್ಲಿ ಟಿಕಟುಬರುಟ ಗುನ್ನೆದಾರ ಜನಾಂಗವೆಂದು. ಇವರನ್ನು ಸರಕಾರವು ಗಣಿಸಿ ಕ್ರಿಮಿನಲ್ ಟ್ರಾಯಿಬ್ಸ್ ಎಂದು ಸೆಟಲ್ಮೆಂಟಿನಲ್ಲಿ ಕೆಲವು ಕಾಲ ಇಟ್ಟಿತ್ತು. ಇದರಲ್ಲಿ ಉಲ್ಲೇಖಿವಾದಂತೆ, ಬ್ರಿಟೀಶ್ ಅಧಿಕಾರದ ಕ್ರಮವು ಹಳೆಯ ಪದ್ಧತಿಯೊಂದಿಗೆ ಹೊಸ ಪದ್ಧತಿಯು ಸೇರಿಕೊಂಡುದರ ಫಲವಾಗಿ ಗ್ರಾಮೀಣ ಜನರು ತಲ್ಲಣಗಳಿಂದ ಬದುಕುವಂಥ ಸ್ಥಿತಿಯು ನಿರ್ಮಾಣಗೊಂಡಿತು. ಕಲಿತವರಿಗೆ ಪರಂಪರೆ ಅನ್ನುವುದು ಅನುಮಾನ ಹುಟ್ಟಿಸಿತು. ಆದರೆ ಸಾಮಾನ್ಯ ಜನರು ಪರಂಪರೆ ಮತ್ತು ಸಂಪ್ರದಾಯಗಳೊಂದಿಗೆ ಬದುಕುವಂಥ ಸ್ಥಿತಿಯು ನಿರ್ಮಾಣಗೊಂಡಿತು. ಜಾತಿ–ಮತಗಳನ್ನು ರಾಷ್ಟ್ರವನ್ನು ರಾಷ್ಟ್ರವನ್ನು ಕಟ್ಟಬೇಕೆನ್ನುವುದು ವಿದ್ಯಾವಂತ ವರ್ಗದ ಒಂದು ಮಾನಸಿಕ ಸ್ಥಿತಿ. ತೊಲಗಿಸಿ ಮತದ ಅಂಧಕಾರವನ್ನು ಎನ್ನುವುದು ವಿದ್ಯಾವಂತ ಜನರ ಒಂದು ಮಾನಸಿಕ ಸ್ಥಿತಿ, ವಿದ್ಯಾವಂತ ಜನರು ಸಾಂಸ್ಕೃತಿಕ ವೈವಿಧ್ಯತೆಗಳನ್ನು ತಮ್ಮ ಬರಹದೊಳಗೆ ತಂದು, ತಾಯಿನಾಡು ಎಂದರೇನು ಎಂಬುದನ್ನು ಬೇರೆ ಬೇರೆ ರೀತಿಯಲ್ಲಿ ನಿರೂಪಿಸಲು ತೊಡಗಿದರು. ಅಷ್ಟೇ ಹೊಸ ರೀತಿಯ ಸಾಂಸ್ಕೃತಿಕ ಪರಿಕಲ್ಪನೆಗಳು ಹುಟ್ಟಿಕೊಂಡವು. ಇದು ಎಷ್ಟರ ಮಟ್ಟಿಗೆ ಮುಂದೆ ಬಂತೆಂದರೆ, ಸಂಪ್ರದಾಯ, ಆಚರಣೆ, ಮೌಲ್ಯಗಳನ್ನು ಹೊಸ ಸಂದರ್ಭದೊಂದಿಗೆ ವ್ಯಾಖ್ಯಾನಿಸಬೇಕಾಗಿ ಬಂತು. ಇದು ಚಾರಿತ್ರಿಕ ಅನಿವಾರ್ಯತೆಯಾಯಿತು. ಇದರೊಂದಿಗೆ ನಗರ ಕೇಂದ್ರಿತ ಬುದ್ಧಿ ಜೀವಿಗಳು (Urban Central Intellectuals) ವಿದ್ಯೆ, ಬುದ್ಧಿವಂತಿಕ (ಈ ಬುದ್ಧಿವಂತಿಕೆಯು ಬ್ರಿಟೀಶ್ ಆಢಳಿತದ ಫಲವಾಗಿ ಹುಟ್ಟಿಕೊಂಡವು ಮತ್ತು ಪಶ್ಚಿಮದ ಚಿಂತನೆಯ ಕ್ರಮದಲ್ಲಿ ತಮ್ಮ ವ್ಯಕ್ತಿತ್ವ ರೂಪಿಸಿಕೊಂಡವರು) ಭಾರತವನ್ನು, ಪ್ರದೇಶವನ್ನು ನೋಡಿದ ಕ್ರಮ ಒಂದು ರೀತಿಯಾದರೆ, ಭಾರತದ ಗ್ರಾಮೀಣ ಜನರು ಬೇರೆ ರೀತಿಯಲ್ಲಿ ನೋಡಬೇಕಾಯಿತು. ಇದು ಕೊಂಚ ಜಟಿಲವಾದ ಸಾಂಸ್ಕೃತಿಕ ಪ್ರಶ್ನೆ. ಒಂದು ಕಡೆಯಿಂದ ಈ ರೀತಿಯ ಚಿಂತನೆಯ

ಹುಟ್ಟಿಕೊಂಡರೆ ವಿದೇಶಿ ಆಡಳಿತದ ಕೆಟ್ಟ ನೀತಿಯ ವಿರುದ್ಧ ದೇಶೀಯ ತುಂಬಾ ಒಳ್ಳೆಯ ಸಂಪ್ರದಾಯಗಳನ್ನು ಪುನರ್ ಪ್ರತಿಪಾದಿಸುವುದು ಸೂಕ್ತವೆಂದು ಪರಿಭಾವಿಸಿದರು. ಕನ್ನಡ ಅತ್ಯುತ್ತಮ ಉದಾಹರಣೆಯೆಂದರೆ ಕುವೆಂಪು ಬರಹಗಳು.

NEP 2020–ಸವಾಲುಗಳು ಮತ್ತು ಅವಕಾಶಗಳು

ಡಾ. ಗುರುಸ್ವಾಮಿ ಹಿರೇಮಠ

ಸಹ ಪ್ರಾಧ್ಯಾಪಕರು, ಕನ್ನಡ ವಿಭಾಗ, ಸರಕಾರಿ ಪ್ರಥಮ ದರ್ಜೆ ಕಾಲೇಜು, ನವನಗರ, ಬಾಗಲಕೋಟೆ.

Email: hiremathggs@gmail.com

ಸಾರಾಂಶ

ಭಾರತ ಸ್ವಾತಂತ್ರ್ಯ ನಂತರ ಒಂದು ಪ್ರಜಾತಂತ್ರ ದೇಶವಾಗಿ ತನ್ನನ್ನು ಆಂತರಿಕವಾಗಿ ಮತ್ತು ಬಾಹ್ಯವಾಗಿ ಕಟ್ಟಿಕೊಳ್ಳುವ ಮತ್ತು ಅಂತರಾಷ್ಟ್ರೀಯ ಮಟ್ಟದಲ್ಲಿ ತನ್ನ ಅಸ್ಮಿತೆಯನ್ನು ರುಜುವಾತು ಪಡಿಸುವ, ಹೆಚ್ಚಿಸಿಕೊಳ್ಳುವ ಅನಿವಾರ್ಯತೆಯನ್ನು ಪ್ರತಿಕ್ಷಣವೂ ಎದುರಿಸುತ್ತಲೇ ಬರುತ್ತಿದೆ. ಅದರಲ್ಲೂ ಬಹು ಭಾಷೆಯ, ಸಂಸ್ಕೃತಿ, ಧಾರ್ಮಿಕ ವಿಚಾರಧಾರೆಗಳು, ನಂಬಿಕೆಗಳು, ರೂಢಿ–ಸಂಪ್ರದಾಯಗಳು ಮತ್ತು ವೈವಿಧ್ಯಮಯವಾಗಿರುವ ಭೌಗೋಳಿಕ ಪರಿಸರದಂತಹ ಅಂಶಗಳು ಪ್ರತಿಯೊಂದು ಯೋಜನೆ ಮತ್ತು ನೀತಿ–ನಿರೂಪಣೆಗಳ ಮೇಲೆ ಪರಿಣಾಮ ಬೀರುವ ಕಾರಣ ಈ ಎಲ್ಲ ಸಂಗತಿಗಳನ್ನು ಅನುಲಕ್ಷಿಸುವ ಮತ್ತು ಕಾರ್ಯಯೋಜನೆಗಳನ್ನು ಪರಿಣಾಮಕಾರಿಯಾಗಿ ಜಾರಿಗೆ ತರುವ ಜವಾಬ್ದಾರಿಗಳನ್ನು ಇದುವರೆಗೆ ಅಲ್ಲಿಕೆ ಮಾಡುತ್ತಾ ಬಂದಿರುವ ಸರಕಾರಗಳು ನಿಭಾಯಿಸುತ್ತಾ ಬಂದಿವೆ. ಈ ಎಲ್ಲ ವಿಚಾರಗಳ ಫಲವಾಗಿ ಈಗಾಗಲೇ ಸಾಮಾಜಿಕ, ಸಾಂಸ್ಕೃತಿಕ, ಆರ್ಥಿಕ ಮತ್ತು ಶೈಕ್ಷಣಿಕ ನೀತಿ–ಆಯೋಗಗಳನ್ನು ರಚಿಸುವ ಮೂಲಕ ಕಾಲಕಾಲಕ್ಕೆ ಆಗಿರುವ ಮತ್ತು ಆಗುತ್ತಿರುವ ಬದಲಾವಣೆಗಳನ್ನಾಧರಿಸಿ ಅನೇಕ ಕ್ರಮಗಳು ಮತ್ತು ಉಪಕ್ರಮಗಳು ಜಾರಿಯಲ್ಲಿವೆ. ಅದರಲ್ಲೂ ಹೊಸ ಹೊಸ ಸವಾಲುಗಳನ್ನು ಎದುರಿಸುತ್ತಿರುವ ಭಾರತೀಯ ಶಿಕ್ಷಣ ಕ್ಷೇತ್ರವು ಮಗುವಿನ ಕ್ರಿಯಾಶೀಲತೆ, ಸೃಜನಶೀಲತೆ, ಅನುಭವಗಳು, ಆತ್ಮವಿಶ್ವಾಸ ಮತ್ತು ಮನೋಬಲವನ್ನು ಹೆಚ್ಚಿಸುತ್ತಾ ಬದುಕಿನ ಸವಾಲುಗಳನ್ನು ಎದುರಿಸುವ ಮತ್ತು ಸರ್ವಾಂಗೀಣ ವಿಕಾಸದ ಆಶಯದೊಂದಿಗೆ ಜೀವನ ಮಟ್ಟವನ್ನು ಇನ್ನಷ್ಟು ಉತ್ತಮಗೊಳ್ಳು ಇವನ ಪ್ರಯತ್ನ ಅವ್ಯಾಹತವಾಗಿ ಸಾಗಲು ಬೇಕಾದ ಸಂಗತಿಗಳ ಶೋಧವು ನಡೆಯುತ್ತಲೇ ಇದೆ. ಆದರೂ ವೈಯಕ್ತಿಕ ಮತ್ತು ಸಮೂಹದಲ್ಲಿ ಬಂದರೆಗುವ ಸವಾಲುಗಳು ಒಮ್ಮೊಮ್ಮೆ ಆತನ ಮನೋಬಲವನ್ನು ಕುಗ್ಗಿಸುವ, ಆತ್ಮವಿಶ್ವಾಸವನ್ನು ನಾಶಗೊಳಿಸುವ ಸಂಗತಿಗಳು ಘಟಿಸುತ್ತವೆ. ಆದಾಗ್ಯೂ ಮತ್ತೆ ಅಂತಹ ಸಂದರ್ಭಗಳಿಂದ ಹೊರ ಬರುವ ಪ್ರಯತ್ನಗಳಂತೂ ನಿರಂತರವಾಗಿ ನಡೆಯುತ್ತಲೇ ಇವೆ. ವ್ಯಕ್ತಿ ತನಗನುಕೂಲವಾಗುವಂತೆ ಈ ಜಗತ್ತನ್ನು/ಸನ್ನಿವೇಶವನ್ನು ತಿದ್ದಲು ಸಾಧ್ಯವಿಲ್ಲವಾದರೂ ತನ್ನ ಮನಃಶಾಂತಿಯನ್ನು, ನೆಮ್ಮದಿಯ, ಆತ್ಮಗೌರವದ ಜೀವನಕ್ಕೆ ದಕ್ಕೆಯುಂಟಾಗುವಂತಹ ಶೋಷಣೆಗಳಿಂದ ದೂರವಿರುವ ಮತ್ತು ಅಂತಹ ಸಂದರ್ಭಗಳನ್ನು ಎದುರಿಸುವ ಮಾರ್ಗಗಳನ್ನು ಶೋಧಿಸುವ ಪ್ರಯತ್ನವೇ ಶಿಕ್ಷಣದ ಹೆಸರಿನಲ್ಲಿ ಆತನನ್ನು ಮುನ್ನಡೆಸುತ್ತಿದೆ. ಅಲ್ಲದೇ ಅದುವೇ ಪ್ರತಿಕ್ಷಣವೂ ಮಗುವಿನ/ಮನುಷ್ಯನಲ್ಲಿ ಹೊಸ ಹೊಸ ಚೈತನ್ಯಕ್ಕೆ ಪ್ರೇರೇಪಿಸುತ್ತದೆ. ಹೀಗೆ ಪ್ರೇರೇಪಿಸುವ ಶಿಕ್ಷಣ ವ್ಯವಸ್ಥೆಯೂ ಅನೇಕ ಸವಾಲುಗಳಿಗೂ ತಂದು ನಿಲ್ಲಿಸುವ ಮತ್ತು ಹೊಸ ಸಮಸ್ಯೆಗಳಿಗೆ ಸಾಕ್ಷಿಯಾಗಿಸುವ ಸಂದರ್ಭಗಳನ್ನೂ ಹುಟ್ಟುಹಾಕುತ್ತದೆ. ಹೀಗಾಗಿ ಇವತ್ತು ಮಗುವಿನ ಶಿಕ್ಷಣವು ಪ್ರಾಥಮಿಕ ಶಿಕ್ಷಣದೊಂದಿಗೆ ಪ್ರಾರಂಭವಾಗಿ ಪ್ರೌಢ, ಪದವಿ–ಪೂರ್ವ, ಸ್ನಾತಕ, ಸ್ನಾತಕೋತ್ತರ ಮತ್ತು ವೃತ್ತಿಪರವಾದ ಪದವಿಯೊರಗಿನ ಶಿಕ್ಷಣದ ಆದ್ಯತೆಗಳನ್ನು ಆಧರಿಸಿ ಸವಾಲುಗಳನ್ನು ಮತ್ತು ಪರಿಹಾರಗಳನ್ನು ಹುಟ್ಟುಹಾಕುತ್ತಿರುವ ಪ್ರಮುಖ ಕ್ಷೇತ್ರವಾಗಿದೆ.

ಅದರಲ್ಲೂ ಬದಲಾಗುತ್ತಿರುವ ಕಾಲಘಟ್ಟದೊಂದಿಗೆ ಹೆಚ್ಚುತ್ತಿರುವ ಜನಸಂಖ್ಯೆ, ವಿದ್ಯಾರ್ಥಿ ಹಾಗೂ ಶಿಕ್ಷಕ ಮತ್ತು ಪಾಲಕರ ಮಧ್ಯ ಹುಟ್ಟಿಕೊಳ್ಳುತ್ತಿರುವ ಹೊಸ ಹೊಸ ಸವಾಲುಗಳು ಒಂದೆಡೆಯಾದರೆ; ಅಸಮರ್ಥವಾಗುತ್ತಿರುವ ಪಾಲಕತ್ವವನ್ನು

ದುರುಪಯೋಗಪಡಿಸಿಕೊಳ್ಳುತ್ತಿರುವ ಯುವಜನಾಂಗದ ಮನೋಧೋರಣೆಗಳು ಇಂತಹ ಸವಾಲಿನ ಸಂದರ್ಭಗಳಲ್ಲಿ ಅದರಲ್ಲೂ ಶಿಕ್ಷಣವೆನ್ನುವುದು ಇವತ್ತಿನ ಎಲ್ಲ ಸಮಸ್ಯೆ ಮತ್ತು ಸವಾಲುಗಳಿಗೆ ಒಂದು ಆಶಾವಾದವಾಗಿ ರೂಪುಗೊಳ್ಳುತ್ತಿದೆ. ಆದ್ದರಿಂದ ಶಿಕ್ಷಣವೆನ್ನುವುದು ಇವತ್ತು ಕೇವಲ ಜ್ಞಾನಾರ್ಜನೆಯ ಮಾರ್ಗವಾಗಿ ಉಳಿದಿಲ್ಲ. ಅದು ಮಗುವಿನ ದೈಹಿಕ ಮತ್ತು ಮಾನಸಿಕವಾದ ಅನೇಕ ಬದಲಾವಣೆಗೆ ತೀವ್ರವಾಗಿ ಸ್ಪಂದಿಸುವ, ವಿದ್ಯಾರ್ಥಿಗಳು ಈ ಶೈಕ್ಷಣಿಕ ವ್ಯವಸ್ಥೆ ಹುಟ್ಟು ಹಾಕುವ ಹೊಸ ಪರಿಸರಕ್ಕೆ ಒಗ್ಗಿಕೊಳ್ಳುವಾಗ ಎದುರಿಸುವ ಪ್ರತಿರೋಧಗಳನ್ನು ಆಧರಿಸಿ ರಾಷ್ಟ್ರೀಯ ಶಿಕ್ಷಣ ನೀತಿ–2020 ಹೊಸ ಹೊಸ ಚರ್ಚೆಗಳನ್ನು ಮತ್ತು ಸಾಧ್ಯತೆಗಳನ್ನು ನಮ್ಮ ಮುಂದಿಟ್ಟಿದೆ. ಈ ಎಲ್ಲ ಅಂಶಗಳ ಹಿನ್ನೆಲೆಗಳನ್ನು, ಪೂರ್ವಾಪರಗಳನ್ನು ಹಾಗೂ ಈ ಶಿಕ್ಷಣ ನೀತಿಯೊಳಗಿನ ಧನಾತ್ಮಕ ಸಂಗತಿಗಳನ್ನು ಮತ್ತು ಆಗಬಹುದಾದ ರೂಪಾಂತರಗಳನ್ನು ಪ್ರಸ್ತುತ ಲೇಖನದಲ್ಲಿ ಚರ್ಚಿಸಲಾಗಿದೆ.

ಅರೆಮಲೆನಾಡು ಪ್ರದೇಶದ ಆಯ್ದ ಪ್ರಾಚೀನ ಶೈಕ್ಷಣಿಕ ಕೇಂದ್ರಗಳಲ್ಲಿನ ಶಿಕ್ಷಣದ ಮೂಲಭೂತ ತತ್ವಗಳು ಹಾಗೂ ಹೊಸ ರಾಷ್ಟ್ರೀಯ ಶಿಕ್ಷಣ ನೀತಿಯ ಮೂಲಭೂತ ತತ್ವಗಳ ನಡುವಿನ ಸಾಮ್ಯತೆಯನ್ನು ಕುರಿತ ಅನ್ವೇಷಣಾತ್ಮಕ ಅಧ್ಯಯನ" (ಕ್ರಿ.ಶ.450 ರಿಂದ ಕ್ರಿ.ಶ.1565ವರೆಗೆ)

ಕೋಟೋಜಿರಾವ್ ಆರ್.

ಸಂಶೋಧನಾರ್ಥಿ, ಶಿಕ್ಷಣ ವಿಭಾಗ, ಕುವೆಂಪು ವಿಶ್ವವಿದ್ಯಾಲಯ, ಶಂಕರಘಟ್ಟ, Email: kotojiraor@gmail.com

ಡಾ. ಎಸ್.ಎಸ್.ಪಾಟೀಲ್,

ಪ್ರಾಧ್ಯಾಪಕರು, ಶಿಕ್ಷಣ ವಿಭಾಗ, ಕುವೆಂಪು ವಿಶ್ವವಿದ್ಯಾಲಯ, ಶಂಕರಘಟ್ಟ, Email: patilss@kuvempu.ac.in

ಸಾರಾಂಶ

ಪ್ರಸ್ತುತ ಅಧ್ಯಯನದಲ್ಲಿ ಶಿಕಾರಿಪುರ ತಾಲ್ಲೂಕಿನ ಅರೆಮಲೆನಾಡು ಪ್ರದೇಶದ ಆಯ್ದ ಪ್ರಾಚೀನ ಶೈಕ್ಷಣಿಕ ಕೇಂದ್ರಗಳಲ್ಲಿನ ಶಿಕ್ಷಣದ ಮೂಲಭೂತ ತತ್ವಗಳು ಹಾಗೂ ಹೊಸ ರಾಷ್ಟ್ರೀಯ ಶಿಕ್ಷಣ ನೀತಿಯ ಮೂಲಭೂತ ತತ್ವಗಳ ನಡುವಿನ ಸಾಮ್ಯತೆಯನ್ನು ಕುರಿತ ಅನ್ವೇಷಣಾತ್ಮಕ ಅಧ್ಯಯನ ಮಾಡುವುದಾಗಿದೆ. (ಕ್ರಿ.ಶ.450 ರಿಂದ ಕ್ರಿ.ಶ.1565 ವರೆಗೆ). ಶಿವಮೊಗ್ಗ ಜಿಲ್ಲೆ ಶಿಕಾರಿಪುರ ತಾಲ್ಲೂಕು ಅರೆಮಲೆನಾಡು ಪ್ರದೇಶದ ಶೈಕ್ಷಣಿಕ ಕೇಂದ್ರಗಳಾದ ತಾಳಗುಂದ, ಬಳ್ಳಿಗಾವಿ, ಬಂದಳಿಕೆ, ಬೇಗೂರು, ಜಂಬೂರು, ಚಿಕ್ಕಮಾಗಡಿ, ಅಗ್ರಹಾರ ಮುಚಡಿ, ಸಂಡ ಹೀಗೆ ಒಟ್ಟು ಪ್ರಮುಖ ಎಂಟು ಶೈಕ್ಷಣಿಕ ಕೇಂದ್ರಗಳಲ್ಲಿ ಲಭ್ಯವಿರುವ ಶಾಸನಗಳನ್ನು ಆಧರಿಸಿ ಈ ಸಂಶೋಧನೆಯನ್ನು ಕೈಗೊಳ್ಳಲಾಗಿದೆ.

ಭಾರತದಲ್ಲಿ ಆದಿಕಾಲದಿಂದಲು ನಡೆದುಕೊಂಡು ಬಂದ ಗುರುಕುಲ ಶಿಕ್ಷಣ ವ್ಯವಸ್ಥೆಯು ಜಗತ್ತಿನ ಅತ್ಯಂತ ಪುರಾತನ ಶಿಕ್ಷಣ ವ್ಯವಸ್ಥೆಯಾಗಿದೆ. ಅಲ್ಲಿ ಆಳವಾದ ಹಾಗೂ ವೈವಿಧ್ಯ ವಿಷಯಗಳ ಅಧ್ಯಯಗಳು ನಡೆಯುತ್ತಿದ್ದವು. ವೇದ, ವೇದಾಂಗ, ದರ್ಶನ, ಪುರಾಣ, ಮೀಮಾಂಸೆ, ವ್ಯಾಕರಣ, ಸ್ಮೃತಿ, ಕಲೆ, ಸಂಗೀತ, ಮೊದಲಾದ ಉನ್ನತ ವಿಷಯಗಳ ಕುರಿತು ಅಧ್ಯಯನಗಳು ನಡೆಯುತ್ತಿದ್ದು, ಗುಣಮಟ್ಟದ ಹಾಗೂ ಉನ್ನತ ವ್ಯಕ್ತಿತ್ವದ ವ್ಯಕ್ತಿಗಳು ನಿರ್ಮಾಣ ಅಂದಿನ ಶಿಕ್ಷಣದ ಮೂಲಭೂತ ಅಂಶವಾಗಿತ್ತು. ಈ ನಿಟ್ಟಿನಲ್ಲಿ ಭಾರತ ಸರ್ಕಾರವು 'ರಾಷ್ಟ್ರೀಯ ಶಿಕ್ಷಣ ನೀತಿ–2020' ಪ್ರಸ್ತುತ ಒಟ್ಟು ಶಿಕ್ಷಣದ ಗುಣಮಟ್ಟವನ್ನು ಸುಧಾರಿಸುವುದು, ಭಾರತವನ್ನು ಜಾಗತಿಕ ಶಿಕ್ಷಣ ಕೇಂದ್ರವಾಗಿ ಗುರುತಿಸಿಕೊಳ್ಳುವುದು ಮತ್ತು ಹೆಚ್ಚು ಸಬಲೀಕರಣಗೊಳಿಸುವುದು ಇದರ ಉದ್ದೇಶವಾಗಿದೆ.

ಪ್ರಾಚೀನ ಭಾರತದ ಶಿಕ್ಷಣ ಪದ್ಧತಿ ಆಧುನಿಕ ಜಗತ್ತಿಗೂ ಮೀರಿದಿತ್ತು. ಶಿಕ್ಷಣದ ವ್ಯವಸ್ಥೆ ಶ್ರೇಷ್ಠಮಟ್ಟದ ಪರಂಪರೆಯನ್ನು ಹೊಂದಿತ್ತು. ಭಾರತದಲ್ಲಿ ಉತ್ಕೃಷ್ಟವಾದ ಶಿಕ್ಷಣ ಸಂಸ್ಥೆಗಳಿದ್ದವು. ವಿಶ್ವವೇ ಅಚ್ಚರಿಪಡುವಂತಹ

ಶಿಕಾರಿಪುರ ತಾಲ್ಲೂಕು ಅರೆಮಲೆನಾಡು ಪ್ರದೇಶದ ಶೈಕ್ಷಣಿಕ ಕೇಂದ್ರಗಳಲ್ಲಿನ ಶಿಕ್ಷಣದ ಮೂಲಭೂತ ಅಂಶಗಳು ಹೊಸ ರಾಷ್ಟ್ರೀಯ ಶಿಕ್ಷಣ ನೀತಿಯ ಮುಂದುವರಿಕೆಯೇ ಆಗಿದ್ದು, ಆಧುನಿಕ ಶಿಕ್ಷಣದಲ್ಲಿ ಬೋಧಿಸಲಾಗುವ ಎಲ್ಲಾ ಶಿಕ್ಷಣದ ಪರಿಕಲ್ಪನೆಗಳನ್ನು ಗುರುಕುಲ ಶಿಕ್ಷಣದಲ್ಲಿ ನೀಡಲಾಗುತ್ತಿತ್ತು. ಭಾರತದ ಶೈಕ್ಷಣಿಕ ಪರಿಕಲ್ಪನೆಯ ಮುಂದುವರಿಕೆಯನ್ನು ಇಂದಿನ ಹೊಸ ರಾಷ್ಟ್ರೀಯ ಶಿಕ್ಷಣ ನೀತಿಯಲ್ಲಿ ಕಾಣಬಹುದಾಗಿದೆ. ಈ ಅಧ್ಯಯನವು ಭವಿಷ್ಯದ ದಿನಗಳಿಗೆ ಮಹತ್ವಪೂರ್ಣವಾದ ದಾಖಲೆಯಾಗಲಿದ್ದು, ಭವಿಷ್ಯತ್ತಿನ ಶೈಕ್ಷಣಿಕ ವಿಚಾರಧಾರೆಗಳನ್ನು ರೂಪಿಸುವಿಕೆಯಲ್ಲಿ ಮಹತ್ವದ ದಿಕ್ಸೂಚಿಯಾಗಲಿದೆ.

ಪ್ರಸಕ್ತ ಕರ್ನಾಟಕದಲ್ಲಿ ಕನ್ನಡದ ಸ್ಥಿತಿಗತಿ

ಡಾ. ಹನುಮಂತಪ್ಪ ಬ್ಯಾಡಗಿ
ಕನ್ನಡ ಉಪನ್ಯಾಸಕರು, ಬಿ.ಎ.ಜೆ.ಎಸ್.ಎಸ್. ಮಹಿಳಾ ಮಹಾವಿದ್ಯಾಲಯ., ಹಲಗೇರಿ ರಸ್ತೆ, ರಾಣೇಬೆನ್ನೂರು,
Email – hibyadgi85@gmail.com

ಸಾರಾಂಶ

ಪ್ರಸಕ್ತ ಕರ್ನಾಟಕದಲ್ಲಿ ಕನ್ನಡವೆಂಬ ಭಾಷೆಯಿಂದಲೇ ಅಸ್ಮಿತೆಯನ್ನು ಪಡೆದುಕೊಂಡಿರುವ ಕರ್ನಾಟಕದಲ್ಲಿ ಕನ್ನಡವನ್ನು ಉಳಿಸಿ ಬೆಳೆಸುವ ಬಗ್ಗೆ ಇಂದು ಆಂದೋಲನಗಳು ನಡೆಯಬೇಕಾಗಿ ಬಂದಿರುವುದು ಕಾಲದ ವಿಪರ್ಯಾಸವೇ ಸರಿ. ಕನ್ನಡದ ಅಳಿವು–ಉಳಿವಿನ ಪ್ರಶ್ನೆ ಬಂದಾಗಲೆಲ್ಲಾ ಶಿಕ್ಷಣದ ವಿಚಾರ ಮುನ್ನೆಲೆಗೆ ಬರುತ್ತದೆ. ಏಕೆಂದರೆ ಒಂದು ಭಾಷೆಯ ವರ್ತಮಾನ ಮತ್ತು ಭವಿಷ್ಯದ ಚರ್ಚೆಗಳಲ್ಲಿ ಶಿಕ್ಷಣ ಮಹತ್ವದ ಪಾತ್ರ ವಹಿಸುತ್ತದೆ. ನಾವು ಶಿಕ್ಷಣದಲ್ಲಿ ಕನ್ನಡವನ್ನು ಬಳಸಬಹೊದಾದ ಸವಾಲು ಹಾಗೂ ಸಾಧ್ಯತೆಗಳನ್ನು ವಿಶ್ಲೇಷಿಸಬೇಕಾಗಿದೆ. 'ಶಿಕ್ಷಣದಲ್ಲಿ ಕನ್ನಡ' ಎಂಬ ವಿಚಾರವನ್ನು ಎರಡು ಆಯಾಮಗಳಿಂದ ನೋಡಬಹುದು. ಮೊದಲನೆಯದು, ಭಾಷೆಯಾಗಿ ಕನ್ನಡವನ್ನು ಕಲಿಯುವುದು; ಎರಡನೆಯದು, ಕನ್ನಡ ಮಾಧ್ಯಮದಲ್ಲಿ ಕಲಿಯುವುದು.ಅನ್ನದ ಭಾಷೆಯಾಗಿ ಕನ್ನಡ ಕುರಿತು ಚರ್ಚೆಮಾಡೋಣ.

ದ್ವಿತೀಯ ಪಿಯು ವಿದ್ಯಾರ್ಥಿಗಳ ಔದ್ಯೋಗಿಕ ಆಯ್ಕೆಗೆ ಸಂಬಂಧಿಸಿದಂತೆ ವೃತ್ತಿಪರ ಮನೋಭಾವ, ವೃತ್ತಿಪರ ಅಭಿವೃತ್ತಿ ಮತ್ತು ವೃತ್ತಿಪರ ಆಸಕ್ತಿ ಕುರಿತು ಅಧ್ಯಯನ

ಡಾ.ಜಾನಕಿ.ಎಮ್,
ಸಂಶೋಧನಾ ಮಾರ್ಗದರ್ಶಕರು, ಸಹಾಯಕ ಪ್ರಾಧ್ಯಾಪಕರು, ಶಿಕ್ಷಣಶಾಸ್ತ್ರ ಅಧ್ಯಯನ ಮತ್ತು ಸಂಶೋಧನಾ ವಿಭಾಗ, ಕರ್ನಾಟಕ ರಾಜ್ಯ ಮುಕ್ತ ವಿಶ್ವವಿದ್ಯಾನಿಲಯ, ಮುಕ್ತ ಗಂಗೋತ್ರಿ, ಮೈಸೂರು.

ಕೆ.ಎಮ್.ಯೋಗೇಶ್,
ಸಂಶೋಧನಾ ವಿದ್ಯಾರ್ಥಿ&ಸಹಾಯಕ ಪ್ರಾಧ್ಯಾಪಕರು, ಜೆಎಸ್ಎಸ್ ಬಿ.ಇಡಿಕಾಲೇಜು, ಚಾಮರಾಜನಗರ,
Email: jssyogi@rediffmail.com

ಸಾರಾಂಶ

ಒಂದು ದೇಶದ ಅಭಿವೃದ್ಧಿಯಲ್ಲಿ ಶಿಕ್ಷಣದ ಪಾತ್ರ ಬಹು ದೊಡ್ಡದಾಗಿದೆ, ಉತ್ತಮವಾದ ಗುಣಮಟ್ಟದ ಶಿಕ್ಷಣವನ್ನು ನೀಡಿದರೆ ದೇಶದಅಭಿವೃದ್ಧಿ ಮತ್ತು ವಿದ್ಯಾರ್ಥಿಗಳ ಭವಿಷ್ಯದಅಭಿವೃದ್ಧಿ ಸಾಧ್ಯ ಹಾಗೂ ಅವರ ಅಧ್ಯಯನದಲ್ಲಿ ಕೌಶಲ್ಯ ಮತ್ತು ಸಾಮರ್ಥ್ಯಗಳನ್ನು ಅಳವಡಿಕೆ ಮಾಡಿ ಶಿಕ್ಷಣವನ್ನು ನೀಡುವುದರಿಂದ ಅವರುಗಳ ಭವಿಷ್ಯಉತ್ತಮವಾಗುತ್ತದೆ ಮತ್ತು

ವಿದ್ಯಾರ್ಥಿಗಳು ಅವರ ಮುಂದಿನ ಜೀವನವನ್ನು ರೂಪಿಸಿಕೊಳ್ಳಲು ಅವಕಾಶ ನೀಡಿದಂತಾಗುತ್ತದೆ. ಆದುದರಿಂದ ಕೌಶಲಗಳು ಮತ್ತು ಸಾಮರ್ಥ್ಯಗಳು ಅತಿ ಮುಖ್ಯವಾದವುಗಳಾಗಿವೆ. ಪದವಿ ಪೂರ್ವ ಶಿಕ್ಷಣದ ಅಧ್ಯಯನದಲ್ಲಿರುವ ವಿದ್ಯಾರ್ಥಿಗಳಿಗೆ ಪದವಿ ಪೂರ್ವ ಶಿಕ್ಷಣದ ನಂತರಅವರ ಔದ್ಯೋಗಿಕಆಯ್ಕೆ ಮಾಡುವಲ್ಲಿ ಅತ್ಯಂತ ಮಹತ್ತದ ಪಾತ್ರವನ್ನು ವಹಿಸುತ್ತದೆ ಆದುದರಿಂದ ಈ ಹಂತದಲ್ಲಿ ವಿದ್ಯಾರ್ಥಿಗಳಿಗೆ ಅವರ ಕೌಶಲಗಳು ಮತ್ತು ಸಾಮರ್ಥ್ಯಗಳು ಅತಿ ಮುಖ್ಯವಾಗಿರುತ್ತದೆ. ಭವಿಷ್ಯದಲ್ಲಿ ವೃತ್ತಿಯ ಆಯ್ಕೆಯಕೂಡ ಒಂದುಸವಾಲಾಗಿದೆ. ವಿದ್ಯಾರ್ಥಿಗಳು ತಾವುಅಧ್ಯಾಯ ಮಾಡುತ್ತಿರುವಾಗಲೇ, ಅವರ ಮುಂದಿನ ಉದ್ಯೋಗಗಳ ಆಯ್ಕೆಗಳ ಬಗ್ಗೆ ಚಿಂತನೆಗಳನ್ನು ರೂಪಿಸಿಕೊಳ್ಳಲು ಮತ್ತು ಆಯ್ಕೆಯ ಸಂದರ್ಭದಲ್ಲಿ ಉತ್ತಮವಾದ ಉದ್ಯೋಗಗಳ ಆಯ್ಕೆಗೆ ಕೌಶಲಗಳು ಮತ್ತು ಸಾಮರ್ಥ್ಯಗಳು ಪ್ರಭಾವವನ್ನು ಬೀರುತ್ತವೆ. ವಿದ್ಯಾರ್ಥಿಗಳಿಗೆ ಈ ಹಂತದಲ್ಲಿ ಕೌಶಲಗಳು ಮತ್ತು ಸಾಮರ್ಥ್ಯಗಳನ್ನು ಬೆಳೆಸುವುದು ಅತ್ಯಂತ ಅವಶ್ಯಕವಾಗಿದೆ. ಈ ನಿಟ್ಟಿನಲ್ಲಿ ಹತ್ತು ಹಲವು ಕೌಶಲಗಳು ಮತ್ತು ಸಾಮರ್ಥ್ಯಗಳನ್ನು ಅವರಲ್ಲಿ ಬೆಳೆಸಬವುದಾಗಿದೆ. ಅವುಗಳೆಂದರೆ ವಿಮರ್ಶಾತ್ಮಕಚಿಂತನೆ: ಭವಿಷ್ಯದ ಕೆಲಸದ ಮೂಲಭೂತ ಕೌಶಲವಾಗಿದೆ, ಸಂವಹನ: ಭವಿಷ್ಯದ ಹಾದಿಯಲ್ಲಿ ಸಂವಹನವು ಪರಿಣಾಮಕಾರಿಯಾಗಿದೆ, ಡಿಜಿಟಲ್ ಸಾಕ್ಷರತೆ: ಉದ್ಯೋಗದ ಆಯ್ಕೆಯಲ್ಲಿ ಪ್ರಮುಕವಾಗಿದೆ. ಸೃಜನಶೀಲತೆ ಮತ್ತು ನಾವಿನ್ಯತೆ: ಸ್ಪರ್ಧಾತ್ಮಕಚಿಂತನೆ ಮಾಡಿಸುತ್ತದೆ, ಭಾವನಾತ್ಮಕ ಬುದ್ಧಿವಂತಿಕೆ: ಭವಿಷ್ಯದ ನಿರ್ವಹಣೆಯನ್ನು ತಿಳಿಸಿಕೊಡುತ್ತದೆ. ತಂತ್ರಜ್ಞಾನ: ಜೀವನದ ಅವಿಭಾಜ್ಯ ಅಂಗವಾಗಿದೆ ಭವಿಷ್ಯವನ್ನುರೂಪಿಸಲು ಅನುಕೂಲವಾಗಿದೆ, ಹೊಂದಾಣಿಕೆಯಚಿಂತನೆ: ಭವಿಷ್ಯದಲ್ಲಿ ಹೊಂದಾಣಿಕೆಯ ಅತ್ಯಂತ ಪ್ರಮುಖಿವಾದುದು, ಪೌರತ್ವ: ಭವಿಷ್ಯದ ದಾರಿದೀಪವಾಗಿದೆ, ಸಾಂಸ್ಕೃತಿಕಅರಿವು: ಭವಿಷ್ಯದಲ್ಲಿ ಜಾಗ್ರತೆಯನ್ನು ಬೆಳೆಸುತ್ತದೆ, ಹೊಂದಿಕೊಳ್ಳುವಿಕೆ: ವಿದ್ಯಾರ್ಥಿಗಳಲ್ಲಿ ಆತ್ಮವಿಶ್ವಾಸವನ್ನು ಮೂಡಿಸುತ್ತದೆ, ಸಕ್ರಿಯೇಕಲಿಕೆ: ಭವಿಷ್ಯದಲ್ಲಿ ಉತ್ತಮ ಮಾರ್ಗವನ್ನು ಪಡೆಯಬಹುದು, ಈ ಮೇಲಿನವುಗಳಲ್ಲದೆ ಇನ್ನೂ ಹತ್ತು ಹಲವಾರು ಕೌಶಲಗಳು ಮತ್ತು ಸಾಮರ್ಥ್ಯಗಳು ವಿದ್ಯಾರ್ಥಿಗಳ ಭವಿಷ್ಯವನ್ನು ರೂಪಿಸುತ್ತದೆ, ಆದುದರಿಂದಾಗಿ ವಿದ್ಯಾರ್ಥಿಗಳಿಗೆ ಈ ಹಂತದಲ್ಲಿ ಅವರ ಭವಿಷ್ಯವನ್ನು ಉತ್ತಮಪಡಿಸಲು ಮತ್ತು ಅಳವಡಿಸಿಕೊಳ್ಳಲು ಉತ್ತಮವಾದ ಅವಕಾಶಗಳನ್ನು ಮಾಡಿಕೊಡುವುದು ಒಂದು ವ್ಯವಸ್ಥೆಯ ಬಹು ಮುಖ್ಯಕಾರ್ಯವಾಗಿದೆ ಎಂದು ಹೇಳಬಹುದಾಗಿದೆ. ಈ ಅಧ್ಯಯನದಿಂದ ದ್ವಿತೀಯ ಪಿಯು ವಿದ್ಯಾರ್ಥಿಗಳಲ್ಲಿ ಔದ್ಯೋಗಿಕ ಆಯ್ಕೆಯಲ್ಲಿ ಇರುವ ಮನೋಭಾವ, ಮನೋವೃತ್ತಿ ಮತ್ತು ಆಸಕ್ತಿಯನ್ನು ಕುರಿತು ಅಧ್ಯಯನ ಮಾಡುವುದೇ ಈ ಅಧ್ಯಯನದ ಮಹತ್ತ್ವವಾಗಿದೆ.

ಗ್ರಾಮೀಣ ವಿದ್ಯಾರ್ಥಿಗಳ ಶಿಕ್ಷಣದ ಮೇಲೆ ಡಿಜಿಟಲ್ ತಂತ್ರಜ್ಞಾನದ ಪ್ರಭಾವದ ಕುರಿತು ಒಂದು ಅಧ್ಯಯನ

ಶ್ರೀಮತಿ. ಜಯಶ್ರೀ ಕೆಂಗೇರಿ

ಸಂಶೋಧನಾ ವಿದ್ಯಾರ್ಥಿ, ಶಿಕ್ಷಣಶಾಸ್ತ್ರ ಅಧ್ಯಯನ ವಿಭಾಗ, ರಾಣಿ ಚನ್ನಮ್ಮ ವಿಶ್ವವಿದ್ಯಾಲಯ, ಬೆಳಗಾವಿ,

Email: jayashreekengeri79@gmail.com

ಸಾರಾಂಶ

ಡಿಜಿಟಲ್ ತಂತ್ರಜ್ಞಾನವು ಶಿಕ್ಷಣ ಕ್ಷೇತ್ರವನ್ನಷ್ಟೇ ಅಲ್ಲದೇ ಹಲವಾರು ಕ್ಷೇತ್ರಗಳಲ್ಲಿ ತನ್ನ ಪ್ರಾಬಲ್ಯವನ್ನು ಸಾಧಿಸಿರುವುದನ್ನು ಇಂದು ನಾವೆಲ್ಲರು ಸಾಕ್ಷೀಕರಿಸುತ್ತಿದ್ದೇವೆ. ಗ್ರಾಮೀಣ ಪ್ರದೇಶಗಳಲ್ಲಿ, ವಿಶೇಷವಾಗಿ ಭಾರತದಂತಹ ದೇಶಗಳಲ್ಲಿ ಶಿಕ್ಷಣವನ್ನು ಡಿಜಿಟಲ್ ಮಾಡುವುದು ಸುಲಭದ ಕೆಲಸವಲ್ಲ. ಗ್ರಾಮೀಣ ಪ್ರದೇಶಗಳಲ್ಲಿ ಡಿಜಿಟಲ್ ತಂತ್ರಜ್ಞಾನವನ್ನು ಕಲಿಕೆಯಲ್ಲಿ ಅಳವಡಿಸುವುದು ಅನೇಕ ಸವಾಲುಗಳನ್ನು ಹೊಂದಿದ್ದರೂ, ಅತ್ಯಂತ ವೇಗವಾಗಿ ಮತ್ತು ಪರಿಣಾಮಕಾರಿಯಾಗಿ ಬೆಳೆಯುತ್ತಿರುವ ವಿಜ್ಞಾನ ಮತ್ತು ತಂತ್ರಜ್ಞಾನ ಅದನ್ನು ಸಾಧ್ಯವನ್ನಾಗಿಸುತ್ತಿದೆ. ಇಂದಿನ ದಿನಮಾನಗಳಲ್ಲಿ ತಂತ್ರಜ್ಞಾನವು ಜನರ ಜೀವನದಲ್ಲಿ ಒಂದು ಅವಿಭಾಜ್ಯ ಅಂಗವಾಗಿ ಹೊರಹೊಮ್ಮಿದೆ. ಡಿಜಿಟಲ್ ಶಿಕ್ಷಣವು ಭಾರತದಂತಹ ದೇಶದಲ್ಲಿ ಶೈಕ್ಷಣಿಕ ಕ್ಷೇತ್ರದ ಅಭಿವೃದ್ಧಿಗೆ ಹಾಗೂ ಬದಲಾವಣೆಗೆ ಒಂದು

ಪರಿಣಾಮಕಾರಿ ಸಾಧನವಾಗಿದೆ. ಗ್ರಾಮೀಣ ವಿದ್ಯಾರ್ಥಿಗಳಲ್ಲಿ ಕಲಿಕೆಯ ಫಲಿತಾಂಶಗಳನ್ನು ಹೆಚ್ಚಿಸಲು ಡಿಜಿಟಲ್ ಶಿಕ್ಷಣವು ಹೇಗೆ ಪ್ರಭಾವವನ್ನು ಬೀರುತ್ತಿದೆ ಎಂಬುದನ್ನು ಅರ್ಥಮಾಡಿಕೊಳ್ಳಲು ಈ ಲೇಖನದಲ್ಲಿ ಪ್ರಯತ್ನಿಸಲಾಗಿದೆ. ಪ್ರಮುಖವಾಗಿ ಡಿಜಿಟಲ್ ಸಾಕ್ಷರತೆಯನ್ನು ಹೆಚ್ಚಿಸಲು ಮತ್ತು ಅಂತರ್ಗತ ಶೈಕ್ಷಣಿಕ ಅಭ್ಯಾಸಗಳನ್ನು ಹೇಗೆ ಉತ್ತೇಜಿಸಬೇಕೆಂಬುದನ್ನು ಒಳಗೊಂಡಿದೆ. ಪ್ರಸ್ತುತ ಅಧ್ಯಯನದಲ್ಲಿ ಮಾಧ್ಯಮಿಕ ಮಾಹಿತಿ ಮೂಲಗಳನ್ನು ಬಳಸಿಕೊಳ್ಳಲಾಗಿದೆ ಹಾಗೂ ವಿವರಣಾತ್ಮಕ ಸಂಶೋಧನಾ ವಿನ್ಯಾಸವನ್ನು ಅಳವಡಿಸಿಕೊಂಡು ಒಂದು ರಚನಾತ್ಮಕವಾದ ಸಂಶೋಧನಾ ಲೇಖನವನ್ನು ರೂಪಿಸಲು ಪ್ರಯತ್ನಿಸಲಾಗಿದೆ.

ಸಮಕಾಲೀನ ಸಕ್ರಿಯ ಬೋಧನಾ ವಿಧಾನಗಳು: ಅನ್ವಯಿಕತೆ ಮತ್ತು ಕಾರ್ಯಯೋಜನೆಗಳ ಅನುಷ್ಠಾನ

ಡಾ. ವೀರೇಂದ್ರ ಕುಮಾರ ವಾಲಿ ಎಸ್.,
ಸಹಾಯಕ ಪ್ರಾಧ್ಯಾಪಕರು, ಕುಮದ್ವತಿ ಶಿಕ್ಷಣ ಮಹಾವಿದ್ಯಾಲಯ, ಶಿಕಾರಿಪುರ.
Email: veerendrakumarwalis@gmail.com

ಸಾರಾಂಶ

ಬೋಧನಾ ವಿಧಾನಗಳು ವಿದ್ಯಾರ್ಥಿಗಳಿಗೆ ಅಪೇಕ್ಷಿತ ಕಲಿಕೆಯ ಗುರಿಗಳನ್ನು ಸಾಧಿಸಲು ಸಹಾಯ ಮಾಡುವ ವಿಧಾನಗಳಾಗಿವೆ, ಆದರೆ ಚಟುವಟಿಕೆಗಳು ಈ ವಿಧಾನಗಳನ್ನು ಕಾರ್ಯಗತಗೊಳಿಸಲು ವಿವಿಧ ಶೈಲಿಗಳನ್ನು ಬಳಸಿಕೊಳ್ಳುತ್ತವೆ. ಬೋಧನಾ ವಿಧಾನಗಳು ವಿದ್ಯಾರ್ಥಿಗಳಿಗೆ ವಿಷಯವನ್ನು ಚೆನ್ನಾಗಿ ಅರ್ಥಮಾಡಿಕೊಳ್ಳಲು ಮತ್ತು ನಿಜ ಜೀವನದಲ್ಲಿ ಅದರ ಅನ್ವಯದ ಬಗ್ಗೆ ಕಲಿಯಲು ಸಹಾಯ ಮಾಡುತ್ತದೆ.

ಶಿಕ್ಷಕರು ನಿಸ್ಸಂದೇಹವಾಗಿ ನಮ್ಮ ಸಮಾಜದ ಅತ್ಯಂತ ಶ್ರೇಷ್ಠವಾದ ವ್ಯಕ್ತಿಗಳಲ್ಲಿ ಒಬ್ಬರು. ಅವರು ಭವಿಷ್ಯದ ಪೀಳಿಗೆಗೆ ಜೀವನದಲ್ಲಿ ಒಂದು ಉದ್ದೇಶವನ್ನು ಕಂಡುಕೊಳ್ಳಲು ಸಹಾಯ ಮಾಡುತ್ತಾರೆ ಆದರೆ ತರಗತಿಯ ಹೊರಗಿನ ಸ್ಪರ್ಧಾತ್ಮಕ ಪ್ರಪಂಚದ ಸವಾಲುಗಳಿಗೆ ಅವರನ್ನು ಸಿದ್ಧಪಡಿಸುತ್ತಾರೆ. ಬೋಧನೆ ಮತ್ತು ಬೋಧನಾ ಚಟುವಟಿಕೆಗಳು ಎಶಿಷ್ಟವಾಗಿ ಸಾಮಾನ್ಯ ತತ್ವಗಳು, ಶಿಕ್ಷಣಶಾಸ್ತ್ರಗಳು ಮತ್ತು ವಿದ್ಯಾರ್ಥಿಗಳಿಗೆ ಪರಿಣಾಮಕಾರಿ ರೀತಿಯಲ್ಲಿ ಶಿಕ್ಷಣ ನೀಡಲು ತರಗತಿಯಲ್ಲಿ ಶಿಕ್ಷಕರು ಬಳಸುವ ಉಲ್ಲೇಖಿತ ಮಾರ್ಗಗಳಾಗಿವೆ. ಶಿಕ್ಷಕರು ಹಾಗೂ ಪಠ್ಯಕ್ರಮದ ಶೈಕ್ಷಣಿಕ ತತ್ವಗಳು, ತರಗತಿಯ ಜನಸಂಖ್ಯಾಶಾಸ್ತ್ರ ಮತ್ತು ವಿಷಯ ಕ್ಷೇತ್ರಗಳಂತಹ ವಿವಿಧ ಅಂಶಗಳ ಆಧಾರದ ಮೇಲೆ ಇವುಗಳನ್ನು ಆಯ್ಕೆ ಮಾಡಲಾಗುತ್ತದೆ.

ಈ ಪತ್ರಿಕೆಯ ಉದ್ದೇಶವು ಬೋಧನೆಯ ಸಾಂಪ್ರದಾಯಿಕ ವಿಧಾನಗಳು ಮತ್ತು ಬಹು ಮಾಧ್ಯಮಗಳನ್ನೊಳಗೊಂಡ, ಬೋಧನೆಯನ್ನು ಮೌಲ್ಯಮಾಪನ ಮಾಡುವುದು ಮತ್ತು ವಿದ್ಯಾರ್ಥಿಗಳಿಗೆ ಜ್ಞಾನವನ್ನು ನೀಡಲು ಪ್ರಯತ್ನಿಸಬಹುದಾದ ಬೋಧನಾ ವಿಧಾನಗಳನ್ನು ಸೂಚಿಸುವುದು ಮತ್ತು ಚರ್ಚಿಸುವುದು. ಮೂಲಭೂತವಾಗಿ ಬೋಧನೆಯ ಮಾಹಿತಿಯನ್ನು ಕಳುಹಿಸುವ ಮತ್ತು ಸ್ವೀಕರಿಸುವ ಎರಡು ಪ್ರಮುಖ ಅಂಶಗಳನ್ನು ಒಳಗೊಂಡಿರುತ್ತದೆ. ಅಂತಿಮವಾಗಿ, ಒಬ್ಬ ಶಿಕ್ಷಕನು ತಾನು ಅರ್ಥಮಾಡಿಕೊಂಡ ರೀತಿಯಲ್ಲಿ ಜ್ಞಾನವನ್ನು ನೀಡಲು ತನ್ನ ಅತ್ಯುತ್ತಮ ಪ್ರಯತ್ನವನ್ನು ಮಾಡುತ್ತಾನೆ. ಆದ್ದರಿಂದ, ಉದ್ದೇಶವನ್ನು ಪೂರೈಸುವ ಯಾವುದೇ ಸಂವಹನ ವಿಧಾನಗಳನ್ನು/ಚಟುವಟಿಕೆಗಳನ್ನು ಬೋಧನೆಯ ನವೀನ ವಿಧಾನಗಳೆಂದು ಪರಿಗಣಿಸಬಹುದು. ನವೀನ ವಿಧಾನಗಳ ಬಳಕೆಯ ಶಿಕ್ಷಣವನ್ನು ಸುಧಾರಿಸಲು ಮಾತ್ರವಲ್ಲ, ವಿದ್ಯಾರ್ಥಿಗಳ ವಿಷಯಗಳನ್ನು ಸಬಲೀಕರಣಗೊಳಿಸಲು, ಜ್ಞಾನವನ್ನು ಬಲಪಡಿಸಲು ಮತ್ತು ಶೈಕ್ಷಣಿಕ ಸಾಧನೆಯನ್ನು ತಲುಪುವ ಸಾಮರ್ಥ್ಯವನ್ನು ಹೊಂದಿದೆ.

ಶಿಕ್ಷಣದಲ್ಲಿ ಹೊಸ ಪ್ರವೃತ್ತಿಗಳು ಮತ್ತು ಬೋಧನಾವಿಧಾನಗಳು
ಬಿ.ಇಡಿ ವಿದ್ಯಾರ್ಥಿಗಳ ಶೈಕ್ಷಣಿಕ ಸಾಧನೆ ಮೇಲೆ ಬೋಧಕರ ಪ್ರೇರಣಾ ತಂತ್ರಗಳ ಪ್ರಭಾವ ಕುರಿತು ಅಧ್ಯಯನ

ರಿಚರ್ಡ್ ಡಿಕಾಸ್ಟ, ದೇವರಾಜ ಎನ್ ಮತ್ತು ಅಶೋಕ ಎಂ
ಸಹಾಯಕ ಪ್ರಾಧ್ಯಾಪಕರು., ಎಸ್.ಜೆ.ಜಿ ಶಿಕ್ಷಣ ಮಹಾವಿದ್ಯಾಲಯ, ಆನಂದಪುರಂ

ಸಾರಾಂಶ

ಶಿಕ್ಷಣವು ಮಾನವ ಸಮಾಜದ ಅಭಿವೃದ್ಧಿಗೆ ಅವಿಭಾಜ್ಯ ಅಂಶವಾಗಿದೆ, ಮತ್ತು ಅದನ್ನು ಯಶಸ್ವಿಯಾಗಿ ಸಾಧಿಸಲು ಬೋಧಕರ ಪಾತ್ರ ಅತ್ಯಂತ ಮುಖ್ಯವಾಗಿದೆ.ಬೋಧಕರ ಮಾರ್ಗದರ್ಶನ ಮತ್ತು ಪ್ರೇರಣಾ ಶಕ್ತಿಯ ವಿದ್ಯಾರ್ಥಿಗಳ ಶೈಕ್ಷಣಿಕ ಬೆಳವಣಿಗೆಯಲ್ಲಿ ಪ್ರಮುಖ ಪಾತ್ರವನ್ನು ವಹಿಸುತ್ತದೆ. ಬಿ.ಇಡಿ (ಬ್ಯಾಚುರಲ್ ಆಫ್ ಎಜುಕೇಶನ್) ವಿದ್ಯಾರ್ಥಿಗಳು ಭವಿಷ್ಯದ ಬೋಧಕರಾಗಬೇಕಾದ ಕಾರಣ, ಅವರ ಶೈಕ್ಷಣಿಕ ಸಾಧನೆ ಕೇವಲ ಅಕಾಡೆಮಿಕ್ ಮಟ್ಟಕ್ಕೆ ಸೀಮಿತವಲ್ಲ: ಅದು ಬೋಧನೆಯ ತಂತ್ರ, ವ್ಯಕ್ತಿತ್ವ ವಿಕಾಸನ, ಮತ್ತು ಬೋಧನಾ ಮಾರ್ಗದರ್ಶನದ ಮೇಲೂ ಅವಲಂಬಿತವಾಗಿದೆ.

ಪ್ರೇರಣೆ(ಮೋಟಿವೇಶನ್) ಎಂಬುದು ಕಲಿಕೆಯಲ್ಲಿ ನಿರಂತರ ಪ್ರಗತಿಯುಂಟು ಮಾಡುವ ಪ್ರಾಥಮಿಕ ಅಂಶವಾಗಿದ್ದು,ವಿದ್ಯಾರ್ಥಿಗಳಲ್ಲಿ ಉತ್ಸಾಹ, ನಿಸ್ಸಂಶಯ ಹಾಗೂ ನಿರಂತರ ಕಲಿಕೆಯ ಇಚ್ಛೆಯನ್ನು ಉಂಟುಮಾಡುತ್ತದೆ. ಬೋಧಕರು ಉಪಯೋಗಿಸುವ ಪ್ರೇರಣಾ ತಂತ್ರಗಳು,ಅವರ ಬೋಧನಾ ಶೈಲಿ, ಮತ್ತು ವಿದ್ಯಾರ್ಥಿಗಳೊಂದಿಗೆ ಹೊಂದಾಣಿಕೆಯ ಧೋರಣೆಗಳು ಬಿ.ಇಡಿ ವಿದ್ಯಾರ್ಥಿಗಳ ಶೈಕ್ಷಣಿಕ ಸಾಧನೆಗೆ ನೇರವಾಗಿ ಪರಿಣಾಮ ಬೀರುತ್ತದೆ.ಈ ಅಧ್ಯಯನವು ಬೋಧಕರ ಪ್ರೇರಣಾ ತಂತ್ರಗಳು ಶೈಕ್ಷಣಿಕ ಸಾಧನೆಗೆ ಎಷ್ಟು ಪರಿಣಾಮಕಾರಿಯಾಗಿ ಪ್ರಭಾವಿಸುತ್ತವೆ ಎಂಬುದನ್ನು ವಿಶ್ಲೇಷಿಸುತ್ತದೆ.

ಭಿನ್ನ ವ್ಯಕ್ತಿತ್ವಗಳಿರುವ ಬಿ.ಇಡಿ ವಿದ್ಯಾರ್ಥಿಗಳು ವಿವಿಧ ರೀತಿಯ ಪ್ರೇರಣೆಯನ್ನು ಅಗತ್ಯವಿರುವ ಸಂದರ್ಭದಲ್ಲಿ, ಬೋಧಕರು ಅವರ ಅಗತ್ಯಗಳಿಗೆ ಅನುಗುಣವಾದ ತಂತ್ರಗಳನ್ನು ಬಳಸುವುದರಿಂದ,ಕಲಿಕಾ ಪ್ರಕ್ರಿಯೆಯ ಉತ್ತಮ ವಿರ್ವಹಣೆ ಸಾಧ್ಯವಾಗುತ್ತದೆ.ಈ ಅಧ್ಯಯನವು, ಬೋಧಕರ ಪ್ರೇರಣಾ ತಂತ್ರಗಳು ಬಿ,ಇಡಿ ವಿದ್ಯಾರ್ಥಿಗಳ ಶೈಕ್ಷಣಿಕ ಸಾಧನೆಯನ್ನು ಸುಧಾರಿಸುತ್ತವೆಯೇ ಎಂಬುದರ ಕುರಿತಾದ ಮಹತ್ವದ ಹಿನ್ನೋಟವನ್ನು ಒಳಗೊಂಡಿದೆ.